Published by BSA Publishing 2023 who assert the right that no part of this publication may be reproduced, stored in a retrieval system or transmitted by any means without the prior permission of the publishers.
Copyright @ Barry Faulkner 2023 who asserts the moral right to be identified as the author of this work

Cover art by Orphan Print, Leominster
Edited by DPL

The facts and information for this book have been gathered from court transcripts, newspaper reports of the time, various internet pages and police and NCA records where available. Any information that is not correct is apologised for in advance. I do my best to double check everything and will be pleased to correct any errors. The whole book is, as usual in true crime, 'without prejudice'.

The cases in this book are also listed in the UK KILLERS series volumes 1 – 3.

CW01656761

UK

FEMALE KILLERS

1900 – 2021

KEMI ADEYOOLA

1987 – sentenced to life imprisonment (minimum 20years) June 27th 2006

Adeyoola was just 18 when she stabbed 84 year old Anne Mendel to death on the doorstep of the Mendel's home in Golder's Green, London on March 19th, 2005. Adeyoola, a daughter of a millionaire estate agent with a private education, was a prolific shop lifter who had recently been released from Bullwood Hall young offender's institution. Whilst in there she had written an 18 page guide on how to murder elderly rich people to get rich yourself which she entitled 'Prison and After; Making Life Count.' Later at her trial she would say this was a draft for a crime novel. Adeyoola had chosen Anne Mendel as a practice target before searching out a very rich old lady to kill solely for money. She had a target of £3m. Her plan was to stake out houses worth millions of pounds in isolated areas with an elderly female owner. Attack the owner after dark and with the help of a tranquiliser and threats obtain the target's bank account pin number and safe combination if there was one in the house. The victim would then be forced to write a letter to her husband or family saying she was leaving him for somebody else and would then be killed and dismembered into bin bags which would be left a long way away from the area in separate street waste bins.

Adeyoola was caught after the Mendel murder by tiny spots of her DNA on one of Anne Mendel's hands.

She had disposed of all the clothes she had worn for the attack and just that DNA identified her. She told the court that her DNA on Mrs Mendel's hand had probably got there when she helped an old lady across the road that day which might have been Mrs Mendel. At the Old Bailey on 26th June 2006 the jury returned a guilty verdict on the murder of Mrs Mendel and the judge sentenced Adeyoola to life imprisonment with a minimum 20 year term

MARGARET ALLEN

1906 – January 12th, 1949. Hanged.

Margaret Allen would probably be classed at transgender these days. She was a lesbian who dressed in men's clothes, insisted people call her 'Bill', she had her hair cut short, drank excessively in pubs and working men's clubs and took part in sports that were mainly in the male domain that needed strength and stamina. She claimed that she had been into hospital at some stage and had a 'delicate operation' that had made her biologically a male. This is disputed as in the 1930-40s such operations were not being medically performed. She worked as a bus conductor in Rawenstall, Lancashire until being fired due to her acting in a masculine manner which in her mind was to swear, act aggressively and pick fights at any opportunity. Bus customers were shouted at and pushed around if they didn't take their seat quickly or have the correct fare. She had no real friends except Mrs Annie Cook a married neighbour who felt sorry for her loneliness. They had been on holiday together just once where Mrs Cook had been offended by Allen making sexual advances as she had no interest in that side of their relationship. Allen bought the town's old police headquarters in Bacup Road which was in a bad structural condition and lived there alone as a near hermit. Mrs Cook was her only visitor and told the police at a later date that Allen had tried to commit suicide using the coal gas oven at least twice. (natural gas didn't replace the coal gas until the 1970's in the UK).

On August 29th 1948, the body of local widow Mrs Nancy Chadwich, 68 who was known to be unpleasant and ill natured was found on the road outside Allen's house with her head battered. Police at first thought she had been the victim of a hit and run driver but forensics later established the head wounds had been made with a coal hammer. During the detectives appraisal of the crime scene and the surrounding area Allen stood silently by and at one point pointing at the river Irwell which flowed nearby shouting 'what's that?' *'That'* was Mrs Chadwick's bag in which it was well known she carried all her savings. It was retrieved from the water and found to be empty. Allen began to focus the detectives attention on herself over the next few days by often staying in the local pub all day drinking and telling the local press how she had been the last person to see Chadwick alive and how Chadwick was a stupid old woman who sat on a bench counting her money in public near to where her body was found. Their interest being aroused the police visited Allen's house on September 1st with a search warrant and inside the front door found blood stains on the wall plus more in the cellar and a coal hammer with Chadwick's hairs stuck to it. When taken to the police station and charged with Chadwick's murder Margaret Allen confessed but couldn't give a reason for killing the old lady who had knocked on her door and walked inside uninvited to borrow a cup of sugar. At her trial Allen wore male clothes and despite her lawyers' attempts to prove her insane and of diminished responsibility she was found guilty and sentenced to death. Her friend Mrs Annie Cook arranged a petition in the town asking for the sentence to be commuted to life imprisonment but out of 30,000 residents just 162 signed it. Margaret Allen was hanged at Strangeways prison on January 12, 1949.

BEVERLEY GAIL ALLITT

Born October 4th, 1968 – sentenced to 13 concurrent life imprisonment terms on May 28th 1993.

Allitt trained as a nurse at Grantham College Lincolnshire. She had periods of non-attendance and failed her nursing examinations but was still accepted for a nursing position at Grantham and Kesteven Hospital in Lincolnshire in 1991 as a State enrolled Nurse. She was assigned to Children's Ward 4.

On February 21st, 1991 Liam Taylor was just 7 weeks old when he was admitted to the ward with possible pneumonia. The next day Liam's parents visited and were told he had suffered breathing problems during the night but had recovered well. The following night Allitt volunteered for extra night duty. During her shift she was alone with Liam and pressed the emergency button. Liam had stopped breathing and as a consequence had suffered severe brain damage and was kept on a life support machine. His parents made the terrible decision to turn off the machine as there was no chance of any recovery. Although questions were raised as to why the monitoring machine failed to send an alarm when Liam stopped breathing no investigation was made and Allitt was not questioned.

A fortnight later 11-year-old Timothy Hardwick was admitted to Ward 4 with a chest infection. Allitt was his assigned nurse. Within minutes of her attending to him his heart stopped beating. He was unable to recover and his death attributed to epilepsy with no obvious cause found.

On March 3rd, 1991 one year old Kayley Desmond was admitted to Ward 4 with a chest infection. Allitt was assigned as her nurse. Kayley was recovering well and due to be discharged when she inexplicably went into cardiac arrest. She recovered and was transferred to a Nottingham Hospital where during an initial examination doctors noticed an unexplained needle puncture under her armpit and an air bubble. It was put down as an accidental injection sometime previously and never investigated further.

On March 20th, 1991 a five-month-old baby boy with bronchitis was admitted into Allitt's care. Shortly before he was due to be discharged he was found comatose with a high level of insulin in his blood. He suffered these symptoms three more times before being transferred to Nottingham Hospital where on arrival he was found to have high insulin level in his blood. Allitt was the nurse who accompanied him in the ambulance to Nottingham. Thankfully the boy survived.

On March 21st, 1991, five year old Bradley Gibson was admitted to Ward 4 with pneumonia. During the evening under Allitt's watch he suffered a cardiac arrest and was successfully resuscitated. A subsequent blood test found he had a high level of insulin. Back on the ward he was cared for by Allitt and suffered another cardiac arrest. After a further resuscitation he was transferred to Nottingham.

One would have thought others on the ward might have put two and two together by now or at least started asking relevant questions? But no, they didn't and Allitt was free to continue along her murderous path. Seven more helpless victims were killed by Allitt before she was brought to book.

On April 22nd, 1991, fifteen month old Claire Peck was admitted to Ward 4 and Allitt's care after suffering a serious asthma attack. On Allitt's watch she suffered a cardiac arrest and was resuscitated. She was left in Allitt's care and suffered another arrest and this time was not able to be resuscitated. An autopsy was performed and found the drug Lignocaine in her body, a drug given to adults having a cardiac arrest but never to a child or a baby. How the drug came to be administered to Claire was a serious mystery and the police were called in.

Serious crime officers examined the files of 25 suspicious baby and child illnesses on Ward 4, four of whom had died. In most cases they found either unaccountable high levels of insulin or potassium had been recorded in their bodies. The only common factor linking them all was the sole presence of Nurse Beverly Allitt each time.

Allitt was arrested and charged with four counts of murder, 11 counts of attempted murder and 11 counts of causing grievous bodily harm. She was examined whilst on remand by several medical professionals who stated that she exhibited the symptoms of both Munchausen's syndrome and Munchausen's syndrome by proxy. This mental disorder basically involves inflicting injury on others to gain attention for oneself.

She was sent for trial at Nottingham Crown Court on 15th February 1993 and on May 23rd, 1993 Beverly Allitt was convicted of all charges and given 13 concurrent life sentences for murder and attempted murder. She will never be released or allowed to apply to the parole board. She was incarcerated at Rampton Secure Hospital in Nottingham and at the time of writing is still there. The Maternity Unit at Grantham and Kesteven Hospital was closed down. None of the management were disciplined or sacked. Several television documentaries have been made about the case and Allitt has been dubbed by the media as 'The Angel of Death'.

JANE ANDREWS

Born 1967 – sentenced to life imprisonment 16th May 2001.

This murder and the trial was a media sensation in the UK and abroad due to the killer's relationship with Sarah, Duchess of York.

Andrews was the youngest of 3 children born in Cleethorpes, North Lincolnshire in 1967. She was the daughter of a joiner and a social worker who struggled with debt and moved to a smaller house in Grimsby before she reached her teens. Andrews early years were beset with psychological problems of depression, panic attacks and eating disorders. She would walk around the town all day rather than attend school and attempted suicide by an overdose of pills aged 15 after her mother found out about the truancy. At 17 she had an abortion. She enrolled in a fashion course at Grimsby College of Art which led to a job as a children's clothes designer with Marks and Spencer. In 1988 age 21 she answered an advert in Lady Magazine for a personal dresser not knowing it was for Sarah, Duchess of York. She was interviewed by the Duchess and given the job working at Buckingham Palace starting 4 days later at a salary of £18,000. She bought a flat in Battersea Park and wallowed in her new opulent life style. There was an accusation that she stole £250,000 of jewellery from her employer but this was never substantiated or proved.

Andrew's love life progressed as well. In 1990 she married Christopher Dunn-Butler an IBM executive twenty years older than her. They divorced and she had a relationship with Dimtri Horne, the son of a very rich Greek shipping magnate. After a bitter break up she went into deep depression and survived an overdose. Andrews was known to have had a few flings outside her relationships and admitted to them. One in particular with Tuscan aristocrat Count Gaddo della Gheradecsu led to her dismissal as Sarah, Duchess of York was allegedly also in bed with the Count and didn't like the competition! The reason for her dismissal given by Palace officials was 'cost cutting'.

In 1998 she met Thomas Cressman, a former stockbroker and multi-millionaire with a successful car accessory business who moved in the elite social circle and soon she moved into his Fulham flat in Maltings House, Bagley's Lane. She took a job as PR manager at Claridges hotel but left after 2 months, we don't know why?

In September 2000 Andrews and Cressman holidayed at his family's villa on the French Riviera where Andrews had told friends she was expecting a marriage proposal. It never materialised, in fact Cressman told her he had no intention of marrying her. On their return to the Fulham flat the relationship became ugly. On September 17th 2000 Cressman called the police asking for assistance as 'somebody is going to get hurt here'. The police didn't respond and whilst Cressman slept that night Andrews killed him by beating him with a cricket bat and stabbing him before fleeing the scene. She tried to create an alibi by texting friends asking if they knew where Cressman was and that she was out searching for him. Her phone then went dead. Cressman's family discovered the body and some days later the police found Andrews in Cornwall, overdosed in her car. She survived and was arrested for Cressman's murder.

At her trial at the Old Bailey in May2001 Andrews was found guilty of Cressman's murder and sentenced to life imprisonment. In November 2009 after serving 9 years she absconded from East Sutton Park Prison in Kent being recaptured 3 days later in a hotel room with her family just six miles away. No addition was made to her sentence for absconding. On 19th June 2015 she was released on licence to a probation hostel with a view to slowly reinstating her into normal life over a period of time. She was recalled to prison when accused of harassing an old boyfriend but re-released when the claim was unsubstantiated. Now aged 55 her present whereabouts is not known but she was working in an unnamed Morrison's in Lincolnshire in 2021 and may well be still there.

TRACIE MARGUERITE ANDREWS

April 9th 1969 – sentenced to life imprisonment July 29th 1997

On December 1st 1996, Andrews aged 28, a former model attacked her boyfriend Lee Harvey late one evening in his car after he pulled over as they were having an argument on the way home to their flat in The Becks, Alvechurch, Worcester. Harvey was a bus driver with a four year old daughter from a previous relationship. Andrews stabbed Harvey over 30 times with a pen knife and left the car screaming and hysterical to telling the police that Harvey had been killed in a road rage attack by a man who had 'staring eyes' after a wild car chase through the back lanes of Worcestershire. This man was obviously never found and nor were any witnesses to the non-existent attack. Andrews even appeared at a police press conference on December 3rd appealing for the public's help and took a drugs overdose the next day which she survived. She was kept in hospital for observation and arrested for Harvey's murder in her hospital bed on December 7th and charged before being bailed. Evidence of many previous arguments and fights between the pair was presented at court plus forensic evidence pointing towards Andrews as the killer. At the Birmingham Crown Court in July 1997 she continued with her road rage scenario even when under oath. She was found guilty and sentenced to life imprisonment with the judge recommending a 14 year minimum term.

In jail she changed her name to Tia Carter and struck up a friendship with Jane Andrews (see previous listing). She also had a submandibular osteotomy operation to correct her bottom jaw from protruding over her top jaw. Public outcry ensued when it was revealed the NHS paid for this cosmetic operation. . It is understood that she spent the last years of her sentence in Askham Grange open prison in York and was put into a secure hostel in the North of England with a night curfew as she adjusted to normal life. She was released from prison at the end of her sentence in 2011 to start a new life as Tia Carter with the condition that she is prohibited from coming within 25 miles of the Harvey family unless under supervision. In 2017 aged 48 and with another name change to Jenna Stephens she married 56 year old bouncer Phil Goldsworthy in Redruth, Cornwall having met him at the pub where she worked behind the bar.

HEATHER ARNOLD

Born 1936 – sentenced to life imprisonment April 16th 1987

Heather Arnold and Paul Sutcliffe both taught at Kingsdown Comprehensive School in the quiet town of Warminster in Wiltshire. When Arnold's marriage broke down Sutcliffe and his wife, Jeanne, gave the fifty year old Arnold support and help to overcome the situation in any way they could.

Paul Sutcliffe came home from work on 30th April 1986 and found his 39 year old wife and his eight month old daughter battered to death on the floor. The police pathologist quickly established that although both bodies were severely beaten around the head the cause of death in both cases was a cut throat. A search was made in the area for the murder weapon with a team of undercover detectives working alongside the local dustmen and examining each bin as it was emptied in the dust cart. The police had talked to neighbours and were aware of Arnold's repeated presence at the Sutcliffe's house which had been noted and was the subject of speculation of an affair between Paul Sutcliffe and Heather Arnold, which was totally untrue. But, bearing these visits in mind special attention was given to Arnold's rubbish and rightly so as a bag in the bin contained the charred remains of an axe handle, the dimensions of which fitted the wounds on the victims' heads. Heather Arnold was arrested and confessed to the killings on the way to the police station but then withdrew that confession on her solicitors advice.

Arnold was sent to trial on 1st April 1987 at Bristol Crown Court where she stated that for some reason she could not explain she had found the axe in her garage, burnt it in her fireplace and chopped up the remains before putting it in a bag and into the waste bin. She couldn't explain that action. Forensics had found flakes of paint from the axe in her car and on Jeanne Sutcliffe's body. On the 15th April 1987 a unanimous guilty verdict was returned by the jury on two counts of murder and Heather Arnold was sentenced to life imprisonment.

Although a plea of 'diminished responsibility' could have been used at the trial Arnold's defence didn't use it. A Hospital psychiatrist at Broadmoor to whom she admitted that she 'hated' Mrs Sutcliffe and had killed her because she 'wanted to be closer' to Paul Sutcliffe, said in 1993 that she had good grounds for an appeal to ask for a retrial on a charge of manslaughter on 'diminished responsibility' rather than murder. The appeal was made in 1996 and rejected on the grounds that Arnold had been subjected to psychological tests before the trial and shown to be highly intelligent at that time with no relevant abnormalities found and in a fit state to take decisions about her defence and instruct her lawyers.

SUSAN BARBER

1953- sentenced to life imprisonment December 1982.

When Michael Barber 24, married Susan 17, in 1970 she already had an illegitimate daughter from a previous relationship although she told Michael it was his child. He was an unskilled manual worker with past offences and prison sentences for car theft and then added indecent assault of his six year old niece to his record in 1972. The Barbers lived in a pre-war terraced council house in Osborne Road, Westcliff-on-Sea, Essex. By 1980 two more children had arrived in the family and there is dispute as to whether or not they were Michael's. Susan had been carrying on an illicit affair with neighbour Richard Collins aged just 15 throughout the marriage. Collins would sneak into the Barber's house as soon as Michael left for work in the morning. It was so blatant that it was sure to backfire and on Saturday 31st March 1981 it did. Michael rose early at 4am to go on a fishing trip on a boat in the Thames estuary with a few likeminded friends. Due to high winds the trip was cancelled and Michael returned home to find Collins in bed with his wife. He, somewhat understandably, hit them both a few times before physically throwing Collins out into the street half naked. Collins fled the area and stayed with his brother in Southend for two weeks. On the Monday following the incident Susan went to her local doctor for treatment to bruising and cuts. The doctor gave the pair of them ongoing help and advice with their matrimonial problems with both seeming to want to patch things up. Beneath the surface Susan was still secretly in contact with Collins and their relationship deepened. Their home life worsened with neither speaking directly to the other except through their children.

On Thursday 4th June 1981 Michael became quite ill with headaches and stomach pain. By the following Saturday he felt so bad he called off work and went to the doctor who put him on a course of antibiotics which had little effect. His condition worsened and he was taken to Southend General Hospital where he was put in ICU. With the condition worsening he was transferred on Wednesday 17th June to Hammersmith Hospital's specialist renal unit. His condition puzzled doctors who worked on the assumption that he may have been poisoned somehow at work and they sent blood and urine samples for analysis at the National Poisons Centre. A negative result was sent back. Michael Barber died on 27th June 1981 and the pathologist carrying out the post mortem did find paraquat poison in his organs which were removed to be preserved and examples sent for histology reports, which are microscopic examinations of the blood cells. It took until September for the histology findings to be reported back and they indicated Michael had been poisoned and probably with paraquat. An investigation as to why the original samples had given a negative result for poison found that the samples were never sent for analysis due to an administrative staff error and when the doctor concerned made an enquiry the staff covered their error by posting a non-existent negative result. Tissue samples from the preserved organs were quickly sent to ICI, the makers of paraquat and to the National Poisons Unit, both came back as positive. Michael Barber had been poisoned.

Meanwhile Susan was partying. Collins had moved in and a succession of regular drink and drug fuelled sex orgies were taking place at the house. Susan had bought a CB radio to contact other party people and used the call sign 'nympho'. Michael's employers had agreed a £15,000 death benefit for her plus £3,300 annually for each child which had been paid to her in October. She thought everything had been settled and that she had got away with murder once Michael had been cremated in July as any evidence of poisoning would have been cremated as well. She wasn't aware of the pathologist's suspicions and the fact that Michael's organs were sitting in the morgue divulging their secret.

On April 5th 1982 Susan Barber and Richard Collins were arrested, Barber was charged with murder, conspiracy to murder and of administering poison with intent to injure. Collins was charged with conspiracy to murder. Both entered pleas of not guilty. Both were found guilty with Susan barber sentenced to life imprisonment and Richard Collins to two years.

MARY FLORA BELL

May 26th 1957 – sentenced for manslaughter 1968. Released 1980.

In 1968 Mary Flora Bell was just eleven years old when she murdered two boys in Newcastle-upon-Tyne. The first was four year old Martin Brown was found strangled inside an old derelict house at 85 St Margaret's Road on Saturday 25th May 1968 by two boys playing ball who had gone inside followed by Mary Bell and her friend Norma Bell, no relation. When the police were called the girls had to be ordered out of the building. Two days later on May 26th a local nursery school was broken into and three notes left on a desk *'fuch off we murder, watch out' 'we did murder martain brown' 'fuckof you bastard'* Four days after Martin Brown being found Mary Bell knocked at his parent's house and asked if she could see Martin in his coffin. On the 31st May a newly installed burglar alarm at the nursery school was activated and brought the police quickly to the scene where they noted Mary Bell and Norma Bell hanging about near the building. They were both taken to the police station where they denied all knowledge of the previous break in and their parents were called to take them home.

Two months later on 31st July 1968 three year old Brian Howe was found strangled on waste ground adjacent to Scotswood Road. His body had numerous small razor cuts on it. The police interviewed over twelve hundred children to plot Howe's last movements.

Mary Bell and Norma Bell were questioned several times and gave answers to the police questions that changed each time eventually blaming each other for Howe's death with Mary accusing Norma of making the cuts on Howe's body with a razor blade. Norma identified the notes found at the nursery as being written by Mary and both were arrested on the 5th August and charged with the murder Martin Brown and Brian Howe. At Newcastle Assizes on 17th December 1968 Norma Bell was acquitted but Mary Bell convicted of manslaughter on the grounds of diminished responsibility after the court appointed psychiatrists described her as having 'classic psychopathy symptoms and a grave risk to other children.' She was sentenced to be detained at Her Majesty's Pleasure.

The family history of Mary Bell is not very nice. Her mother, Betty, was a prostitute having Mary when she was 16 years old to an unknown father. Mary was led to believe it was Billy Bell a career criminal who was her mother's partner and married Betty sometime after Mary was born. Mary herself claims she was sexually abused as a child being rented out from the age of 5 to paedophiles. She grew up in the depressed Scotswood area of Newcastle where domestic violence and criminal behaviour was common place. This probably accounts for acts of violence and attacks on other children before these two murders that didn't attract much attention. Even her boasts after the killings that *'I am a murderer'* were not taken notice of.

After sentencing Bell briefly made the headlines in 1977when she escaped from Moore Court open prison, where she had been sent a year before, with another girl and two boys and recounted in great detail to the press the sexual activities of the four in their two days of freedom. In 1980 Mary Bell then aged 23 was released from Askham Grange open prison having served 12 years. She had been granted anonymity to start a new life. She had a daughter in 1984, the father is unknown. In 2009 it was reported that she had become a grandmother and the anonymity grant had been updated to include the grandchild. Despite that she has been forced to move at least five times after being identified. She is reputed to have received £50,000 in 2003 for collaborating on a book biography, 'Cries Unheard' with author Gitta Sereny.

CHARLOTTE BRYANT

1904 – July 15th 1936. Hanged.

Charlotte McHugh met Frederick Bryant in Ireland in the early 1920's when he was serving in the British Army. When he left the service they moved to Somerset and married, he was 25 and she was 19. By 1925 Frederick was working as a farm labourer and they were living in a tied cottage at Over Compton, Yeovil with five children, not all had Frederick as their father. Charlotte was a nymphomaniac and ignored the family duties in her never ending quest for new sexual liaisons. Frederick was well aware of this and found it easier to look the other way for the sake of the children and the marriage. Sometime in 1933 one of Charlotte's lovers, a horse dealer named Leonard Parsons moved in to their cottage as a lodger. He was a married man with four children of his own and was frequently away conducting his business. Charlotte made no bones about how wonderful she thought Parsons was in comparison to Frederick and how she wished he was her husband. The farm owners became increasingly embarrassed by Charlotte's extra-marital behaviour and the local gossip around the family and in 1934 sacked Frederick. The family moved to Coombe in Dorset where Frederick took another labouring job. In May 1935 Frederick became ill with stomach pains which the doctor put down to gastro-enteritis, Frederick recovered only to fall ill again in that December. He recovered again but later that month another bout of the illness killed him. A post-mortem discovered the equivalent of 4 grains of arsenic in his body and the police then removed Charlotte and the children from the house into a workhouse at Sturminster Newton whilst they conducted a search of the property. They found an empty arsenic tin in the back yard and traces of it around the house and in Charlotte's coat pockets. Charlotte was arrested and charged with Frederick's murder. She was sent to trial at Dorset assizes, Dorchester on Wednesday 27th May 1936. Testimony at the trial from a number of witnesses indicated that Charlotte's 'sexual favours' could be bought for the price of a glass of stout at the local pub or for a few shillings. It seemed that with five mouths to feed Frederick would turn a blind eye. He had told a neighbour, 'I don't care what she does, four pounds a week is better than thirty shillings' His wage as a cow man was £1.50 a week. A local chemist who had sold the tin of arsenic to a lady who signed the Poison Register with a cross picked out Charlotte in a line-up and her comment to the police that charged her with Frederick's murder that 'I haven't poisoned him, I haven't got any poison' before she had been told that Frederick had died from poisoning sealed her fate. The jury took just one hour to return a guilty verdict and the judge pronounced a sentence of death by hanging with the body to be buried within the confines of Exeter prison. She was hanged there six weeks later at 8am on Wednesday July 15th 1936.

Whilst in the condemned cell she wrote a note in which she said, *'it is all the fault of .... that I am here. I listened to the tales I was told.'* The name of the person is redacted now, so we will never know whose fault she thought it was. She left the sum of 5 shillings and eight pence to her children who were taken into care by Dorset County Council.

EMMA 'Kitty' BYRON

1878 – sentenced to death December 17th 1902, commuted to life imprisonment. In 1907 reduced to 10 years. Released 1913.

Emma 'Kitty' Byron an unemployed milliner's assistant had struck up a relationship with Stock Exchange Dealer Arthur Baker and shared a flat in 18 Duke Street off Portland Place, London. Baker was an alcoholic with a violent streak that often surfaced at home. On 7th November 1902 Byron fled the flat in her nightdress to avoid one of Baker's assaults and took refuge in the landlady's rooms. The next morning the couple were asked to pack up and leave. Baker asked if he might stay if Byron left but the request was refused and he was given one week's grace to find another lodging if Byron went immediately. On the morning of 10th November 1902 Byron bought a strong bladed knife in Oxford Street and then sent a telegram to Baker from the Lombard Street Post Office saying 'Dear Reg, I want you a moment, important. Kitty'

When Baker arrived back at the flat an argument started that developed into a full blown fight outside on the street where passers bye looked on in horror as Byron brought out the knife and stabbed Baker twice. One of the stabs severed his aorta and he died almost instantly collapsing onto the pavement. Byron's trial took place at the Old Bailey on December 17th 1902. The landlady and other witnesses testified to Baker's alcoholism and violent temper and recalled seeing

Byron with cuts and bruises to her face on many occasions. The public had sympathy for her and her defence put in a plea for manslaughter instead of murder. The judge was against this and in his summing up to the jury gave a strong argument for murder. The jury returned a guilty verdict for murder with a string recommendation for mercy. The judge ignored it and sentenced Byron to hang but after a 15,000 name public petition and a strong media outcry the Home Secretary commuted the sentence to life imprisonment. In 1907 this was again reduced to 10 years of which she served 6 before being released.

LOUIE CALVERT

Born 1893 – executed at Strangeways Prison Manchester June 24th 1926.

Louie Calvert was a small, unattractive prostitute who used the name Louie Gomersal when working the streets of Leeds. She attended Salvation Army meetings for the food handouts and they knew her as Louie Jackson. She had a 6 year old son, Kenneth by an unknown father. Under the name Jackson she obtained a live-in position as housekeeper to Arthur Calvert, a night watchman living at 7 Railway Place, Pottery Fields, Leeds who allowed her son to live with her. She and Calvert had an affair and when she lied to him that she was pregnant he married her. There was of course no baby and it was a ruse to force Calvert to marry her. She kept the deception going with padding under her skirts until near the end of the 9 month term when she told him she was going to her sister's in Dewsbury for the birth. She sent him a telegram to tell him she had arrived there safely. There was no sister and Louie had returned back to Leeds after sending the telegram and on 8th March 1926 moved into lodgings with 40 year old widow Mrs Lily Waterhouse in Amberly Road, Leeds with an arrangement that Louie would act as maid and housekeeper in return for free board and lodging. Whilst with Mrs Waterhouse Louie noticed an advert for a baby to be adopted from a teenage unmarried couple and made the arrangement to have the baby with the intention to return to Jack Calvert and pass it off as theirs. The arrival of the baby created arguments between Louie and Mrs Waterhouse as Louie didn't hold to her agreement to housekeep and clean. Mrs Waterhouse also noticed several of her pieces of silverware had disappeared and Louie had pawn shop tickets in her room which pointed to Louie stealing the silverware and pawning it. Mrs Waterhouse visited the local police and told them of the situation. They asked her to return the next day and list a formal complaint against Louie for theft and scheduled a court appearance on 1st April to obtain an injunction. Mrs Waterhouse told Louie what she had done and asked her to pack and leave. On 31st March neighbours of Mrs Waterhouse heard banging coming from the terraced house followed by some shouting and a short while later saw Louie leaving with a suitcase and the baby. She told an inquisitive neighbour who enquired about the noise that the banging was the baby's cot that had fallen over and the shouting was Mrs Waterhouse distraught because Louie was leaving.

On 1st April Mrs Waterhouse failed to turn up to court for the injunction and two detectives visited her house the following day and broke in to find the lady had been hit over the head and then strangled to death with a ligature in a small bedroom with no signs of a struggle. She was barefoot.

Louie was the only suspect and the police soon traced her back to Arthur Calvert's house at 7 Railway Place where she opened the door to them wearing Mrs Waterhouse's boots which were several sizes too big. They searched the house and found more pawn tickets and several pieces of the silverware Mrs Waterhouse had listed as missing. Louie was questioned and said Mrs Waterhouse was confused and often forgot things like asking her to pawn the items in lieu of payment for the housework she had done. She stood trial for murder at Leeds assizes on 5th May 1926 and was found guilty of murder. She claimed then that she was pregnant. Pregnant women were always reprieved. At Strangeways she was examined and although it was just possible she was pregnant it was deemed unlikely and at such an early stage would not cause a problem to execute her. Her autopsy after being hanged showed no pregnancy, it was just another of her falsehoods. Then came a twist. Whilst in the condemned cell she confessed to the murder of John Frobisher in 1922. At that time she went under the name of Mrs Louise Jackson and worked as Frobisher's housekeeper at Mercy Street, Wellington Lane, Leeds. Frobisher's body was found floating in a canal on 12th July 1922 with a wound to the back of his head and the autopsy found he had a fractured skull. The body had been fully clothed except that Frobisher's boots were missing and never found. One of the detectives on the Waterhouse case who was also involved in the Frobisher case recognised the similarity of the missing boots between the two. Why Calvert would steal the boots of her victims is unclear. She was very poor, boots were expensive and necessary. Louie Calvert was hanged at Strangeways Prison, Manchester on June 24th 1926 and buried in the prison grounds.

LINDA CALVEY

(born Linda Welford)

Born 8th April 1948 – sentenced to life imprisonment 12th November 1991. Released 2008.

Linda Calvey, born Linda Welford in Ilford 1948 worked in a paint factory as a receptionist before starting her crime career after meeting armed robber Mickey Calvey when he was on home leave from prison where he was serving an 8 year term. They married when she was 22 and she soon became involved in armed robberies herself wielding a shotgun. Her first conviction for armed robbery of Post Offices resulted in a 7 year prison sentence at Holloway Prison, London being released after serving half that. Mickey Calvey died after he was shot by armed police during a botched robbery on 9th December 1978. After his death she was financially supported by Ronnie Cook, an associate of Mickey Calvey who became too controlling of her life and their relationship floundered to the point that she refused his offer of marriage. Cook was sentenced to 16 years for an armed robbery and she was introduced by another robber Brian Thorogood to Daniel Reece whose son had been killed in a traffic accident whilst he was in prison. Thorogood thought they could support each other not knowing that Calvey was quite glad to have Cook put away. Calvey developed relationships with both Reece and Thorogood. In 1990 Calvey paid Reece £10,000 to kill Ronnie Cook when he was on day release but Reece lost his nerve at the last moment and

Calvey snatched the gun and shot Cook herself. Frankie Fraser another gangster who ran with the Krays said at the time that Calvey killed Cook because she had spent most of his money whilst he was in prison and was afraid of what he would do when he found out..

On 12th November 1991 at the Central Criminal Court both Calvey and Reece were convicted of murder and were sentenced to life imprisonment with a minimum tariff of 15 years. Calvey was released in 2008. Reece is still inside after a serious sexual assault on another inmate.

Since her release on licence Calvey married again to millionaire George Ceasar in Dymchurch in 2009. Ceasar died in September 2015. She has two children from her marriage to Mickey Calvey as well as several grandchildren and great-grandchildren. She has been dubbed *'The Black Widow'* as all her lovers and husbands ended up dead or in prison.

SHARON LOUIS CARR

Born 21st December 1979 – sentenced to life imprisonment 25th March 1997. Sectioned under mental health act 1998 and kept in custody after her tariff expired 2009.

Sharon Carr was born in Belize in 1981 and brought up by her mother and step father, a soldier. After moving to Camberley, Surrey, England, her parents split up and after a brief period of being fostered Carr returned to live with her mother. Her personality changed from being polite and helpful at school to being rude and disruptive. Carr is the youngest female murderer to be sentenced in the UK being just 12 when she committed the murder of 18 year old Katie Racliffe on 7th June 1992. The murder of Racliffe remained unsolved until Carr was given a two year sentence in 1994 for stabbing a fellow pupil at Collingwood College, Surrey and admitted to Racliffe's murder during that sentence. Police retrieved her diaries where she wrote about committing the murder and her pleasure in doing it. The stabbing at Collingwood also took place on the 7th June, the same day as Racliffe's murder two years earlier. Police had sought a male killer in the Racliffe case as the body was naked with multiple stab wounds to the breasts, vagina and anus leading to a suspicion of rape.

On the evidence given by Carr to the police and her diary entries Carr was sent to trial at Winchester Crown Court and convicted of the murder of Katie

Racliffe. She was given a life imprisonment sentence with a minimum tariff of 14 years, later reduced to 12. Carr proved to be a very violent and difficult prisoner launching many attacks on prison staff and other inmates. So much so she was assessed as suffering from schizoaffective disorder, sectioned under the Mental Health Act and transferred out of the prison system to Broadmoor Hospital and then to another secure London Hospital when Broadmoor changed to a male only Hospital. Although her tariff expired on 25th March 2009 she is not eligible to apply for parole or be considered for release whilst sectioned.

In Broadmoor Carr met fellow inmate Robbie Layne who killed his own mother when 17 by gouging out her eyes with a carpet sweeper handle and stabbed her several times in a fit of jealousy over his mother's perceived favouritism of his sister. They married in Broadmoor in 2001. The couple will not be allowed to consummate the marriage whilst serving their sentences.

JANICE CARTER

1982 – sentenced to life imprisonment (minimum tariff 12 years) on April 3, 2012.

Kevin Carter, 30, was found dead, stabbed 19 times in his flat in Sweyn Road, Margate, Kent on 14th October 2011. Kevin had been serving an 180 day prison sentence for motoring offences and had been given early release just a few hours before. He shared the flat with Janice Carter, his ex-wife. They had divorced three years previously but decided to give it another go on his release. That day they had been drinking heavily and playing loud music in the flat when the G4S officials arrived to install an electric monitoring device inside the flat, which was a condition of Kevin's early release, the couple argued as to where it should go with Janice being very unhappy when it eventually went in the bedroom and the G4S officials left and could hear the couple shouting at each other from the street. The neighbours also heard the argument ratcheting up in volume. The shouting ceased and the loud music started again, then at about 9pm it all went silent. This was the time that Janice Carter had left the flat and gone to her sister's home in Zion Place and told her, 'I've killed Kevin. I stabbed him. I think he's dead.'

Her brother-in-law went to the flat and found Kevin lying on the kitchen floor with a knife beside him. Police and ambulance were called but he was pronounced dead.

On trial for murder at Canterbury Crown Court Janice Carter denied murder and claimed she had lived in fear of Kevin's violent temper and an argument had developed into a fight in the kitchen where she had automatically, without thinking, grabbed the knife to defend herself. The prosecution pointed out that Kevin had been stabbed 19 times, including many times after he had fallen to the kitchen floor.

On the 3rd April 2012 the jury of 8 women and 4 men found her guilty of murder and the judge sentenced her to life imprisonment with a minimum tariff of 12 years before she can apply for a parole hearing.

PHIONA DAVIS

Born 1979- sentenced to indefinite detention in Broadmoor September 13th 2004

Phiona Davis, 25, of Green Lanes, was a devotee of the controversial Kabbalah sect, which counts Madonna, Britney Spears and Demi Moore among its followers. On October 13th and 14th 2003 the fashion student stabbed lover Keith Fernandez 58 times and knifed her 81-year-old great grandmother Mary Skerritt 130 times. She was a regular worshipper at the London branch of the Kabbalah Centre, in Stratford Place, Mayfair which had been set up with a £3.65 million grant from Madonna. The court heard that neighbours reported a man screaming inside Davis' home and broke down the door to find her astride her boyfriend's body repeatedly stabbing him in the face. Davis warned them, 'Don't come any closer. I'm going to do it.' Mr Fernandez, of Seven Kings, managed to stagger out of the flat, but he collapsed and died. Davis shouted: "God done good, for this is done through God" and fled the scene. The next day she attacked her great-grandmother, Mary Skerritt, 81, at her home in Spencer Grove, Stoke Newington. Neighbours had called the fire brigade after seeing smoke billowing from the old lady's windows. They found Davis outside screaming: "I am God, I am the benevolent one, burn the demons and burn her."

She held out her hands 'like Jesus' and tried to stop the fire fighters entering the flat shouting at them, 'only God can judge me in the heavens.' Mrs Skerritt was found lying in a pool of blood in the hallway. Crucifixes and the woman's jewellery had been laid out on the floor and a palm cross was left by the front door. Davis had set four fires in the house and all the gas rings were turned on. As she was taken away, she screamed: "You can arrest me, but you can't punish me. Only God can punish me." Later, at Stoke Newington police station, she attempted to strangle herself and smeared crosses on the wall with excrement and blood. She shouted at police "I am the messiah and the king of kings. I will forgive you all." At her trial at The Old Bailey on 13th September 2004 psychiatrists described her as one of the 'illest' people they had ever seen. She was cleared of murder by reason of insanity and sent to Broadmoor for an indefinite period. She can never be freed without permission from the Home Secretary.

JOANNA CHRISTINE DENNEHY

1982 – sentenced to life imprisonment November 18th 2013.

Known as The Peterborough Ditch Murders three male victims were found in Cambridgeshire during March 2013. All three died from stab wounds and all three had dealings with Joanna Dennehy a mother of two whose husband had left her and taken the children with him after she had sunk into a life of drink, drugs and violence. Born August 1982 in St Albans Dennehy told her low life friends that she aspired to a life similar to the American gangster murderers Bonnie and Clyde. She had a target of nine victims, all male. Later when incarcerated she admitted to a psychiatrist that after the first couple of killings she had 'got a taste for it.'

The first victim was Kevin Lee a property developer who was also Dennehy's landlord and lover. His body was found dressed in a lady's sequined dress in a ditch outside Newborough on 30th March 2013. The bodies of two further victims, Lucas Slaboszewski an addict friend of Dennehy and John Chapman a housemate were found dumped near Thorney on 3rd April 2013. All the victims had been stabbed to death. A short while after the killings Dennehy and her friend Gary Richards known as Gary 'Stretch' because of his 7ft3inch height, plus another man, drove to Hereford and stabbed two men chosen at random. The other man was an unwilling traveller and was later cleared of any involvement in the attacks.

At the Old Bailey in November 2013 Dennehy pleaded guilty to all the charges which was a surprise to her legal team and to her sister. They were all under the impression a plea of diminished responsibility would be lodged on the basis of psychiatric reports. When her lawyers asked the judge for a delay to the proceedings so they could talk to her she interrupted them, 'I'm not coming back here just to say the same stuff.' She was held on remand at HM Prison Bronzefield, Surrey for further psychiatric reports that established she was psychopathic, anti-social, sado-masochistic and had borderline personality disorders. Back in court at the Old Bailey on 28th February 2014 she was sentenced to life imprisonment with a full life tariff added due to the fact that she had premeditated each murder. Three men, Gary Richards (Stretch) received a life sentence with a minimum term of 19 years for attempted murder and Leslie Layton, who admitted assisting an offender received a14 year prison sentence for perverting the course of justice. Robert Moore who admitted assisting an offended received a 3 year sentence. It emerged afterwards that the probation service were supervising Dennehy at the time of the murders as she had previously been convicted of assault.

When at HMP Bronzefield on remand pending the Old Bailey trial, Dennehy had plotted an escape in her diary. It involved killing a prison officer, cutting off his/her finger to use to access the biometric door system. This led to her being placed in solitary confinement. In 2019 Donnehy was moved to Low Newton Prison in County Durham. Once there she threatened to kill Rosemary West. West had already been moved to another prison.

NICOLA CAROLINE EDGINGTON

Born 1980 – convicted of manslaughter and held under the mental health act 2006. Released 2009. Re-arrested and sentenced to life imprisonment March 4th, 2013.

Nicola Edgington has a younger brother and sister who she used violence against as a child as well as against her mother. She told police she had been abused by her father as a child. She attended Sackville School at East Grinstead, Surrey. Social care workers pulled from the family and put her into secure care homes several times in an effort to calm her down. She was employed at different times as a hairdresser, shop worker and saleswoman as well as prostitute, pole dancer and drug dealer. At just 17 she miscarried twins after being punched in the stomach during a fight and at 19 was pregnant again and gave birth to a son 3 months prematurely. The boy went into foster care. She married a Jamaican man who was the father and also the father of another son who was also put into care. The father managed to obtain custody and take both the boys to Jamaica.

On 4th November 2005 Edgington visited her 60 year old mother Marion in Forest Row, East Sussex and stabbed her 9 times. She was convicted of manslaughter due to diminished responsibility, having been diagnosed with schizophrenia whilst in custody. At Lewes Crown Court on 23rd October 2006 she was sentenced to be detained indefinitely under the Mental Health Act. After intense treatment and further evaluation she was released with parole conditions in September 2009 and settled into a flat in Greenwich. She sent a message to her brother via his Facebook page in 2011 but he wanted nothing to do with her and rejected her posts reminding her that she had killed their mother and that he had found the body.

On the 6, 7 and 9 October2011 Edgington rang the police several times to ask for help evicting drug users from her flat. The police did not attend. On the 10th October she pleaded with both the police and her mental health advisors to be detained as she was having a psychotic breakdown and could murder again. She was taken to the Queen Elizabeth Hospital in Greenwich and left there to await being admitted by the psychiatric staff. Edgington left the hospital through a door that should have been locked or alarmed and took a bus to Bexleyheath and stabbed two strangers. She bought another knife in Asda and tried to kill 22 year old Kerry Clark who survived when a member of the public wrestled the knife from her and she fled the scene. She then stole a knife from a butcher's shop and stabbed 58 year old Sally Hodkin so viciously she almost decapitated her. Hodkin died at the spot. Edgington's exit from the hospital had been noted and the police were already looking for her. She was arrested within the hour.

On 7th February 2013 at the Old Bailey Edgington was found guilty of the attempted murder of Kerry Clark and the murder of Sally Hodkin. On the 4th March 2013 she was jailed for life with a minimum tariff of 37 years. Despite Edgington's efforts of asking the police and mental health persons to detain her prior to the murders the judge took the view that they were premeditated.

SARA EGE

1979 – sentenced to life imprisonment with 17 year minimum January 7th, 2013.

This is religious fervour gone mad! Sara Ege saw a way to climb the social ladder within the Muslim community of Cardiff, Wales, by having her seven year old son, Yaseen, memorise the Koran and become a hafiz, a Muslim who could recite the whole of the Koran from memory. Yaseen would be taught the Koran's words before and after school. However, Sara became angry at Yaseen's inability to memorise whole passages each day and took to beating him with her fists and sticks. Yaseen's school teachers were concerned by his bruises but he always gave a reason for them.

On the day in July that Yaseen died his mother had kept him home from school to focus on reading and memorising the Koran and became frustrated at his lack of memory. She beat him with a rolling pin and he collapsed on the floor. His mother dragged him to his bedroom and left him. When she returned he was dead. To cover her tracks Sara set fire to the house using a barbecue accelerant which she also poured over Yaseen's body. Pathology reports on Yaseen's body showed he died before the fire engulfed his body and that he had broken ribs, a fractured arm and finger amongst other injuries. Traces of the accelerant were found on Yaseen's clothing and hands. At Cardiff Crown Court Sara's assertions that her husband was responsible because he had threatened to kill her if

Yaseen didn't learn the Koran were dismissed by the judge who sentenced her to life imprisonment with a 17 year minimum tariff for the murder of Yaseen and trying to pervert the course of justice.

RUTH ELLIS

October 9th 1926 – July 13th 1955 executed by hanging at Holloway Prison.

Ruth Ellis was the last lady to be executed in the UK. A favourite question in pub quizzes! She was born in Rhyl, S Wales in 1926, the third of six children of a Belgium mother and English father, Arthur Hornby, a cellist who was away a lot playing in Atlantic Cruise Liner orchestras. The family moved to Basingstoke where Ruth left school at 14 to work as a waitress. In 1941 the family moved again to London. In 1944 Ruth had a son, the father was a Canadian soldier who sent her money for a couple of years after returning to Canada where he already had a family. Then the money stopped and Ruth's mother took charge of the boy. In the pursuit of money Ruth gave up the clerical work she was doing and became a night club hostess at the Court Club in Duke Street where she caught the eye of Morris Conley, the owner and was introduced to wealthy patrons and took to prostitution becoming pregnant in 1950 which she had terminated illegally. On 8th November 1950 Ruth married Court Club regular, George Ellis, a divorced dentist with two sons from Tonbridge, Kent. The marriage was a disaster with Ellis being a violent alcoholic who believed Ruth was having an affair. The marriage stumbled on and Ruth became pregnant in 1951and gave birth to a daughter, Georgina, who Ellis refused to accept as his child and they separated soon after the child's birth. Ruth and the child moved back with her parents and Ruth went back to hostessing. In 1953 she was promoted to manager of the Carroll nightclub mixing with celebrities and taking various wealthy lovers who showered her with expensive gifts. She took up with racing driver David Blakely who was three years younger than her and moved into her flat above the nightclub. Blakely was already engaged to another woman at the time, Mary Dawson. The relationship with Ruth floundered and she began an affair with ex RAF pilot Desmond Cussens whose family owned a wholesale and retail tobacco company with multiple outlets in London and S Wales. Ruth was sacked as manager of the Carroll Club and moved in with Cussens at 20 Goodward Court, Devonshire Street, off Oxford Street. She also continued her relationship with Blakely despite both having various other relationships on the side. Ruth lost another child when Blakely punched her in stomach after being told she was pregnant. Their relationship became nasty and violent. On 10th April 1955, Easter Sunday, Ruth Ellis took a cab from Cussens's home to 29 Tanza Road, Hampstead, the home of Anthony and Carole Findlater, close friends of Blakely. She arrived as Blakely drove off. Ruth walked the short distance to the Magdala public house in South Hill Park, Hampstead, a favourite drinking hole of Blakely's and found his car in the car park. Ruth waited in the doorway of a news agents next to the pub until Blakely and a mutual friend, Clive Gunnell, emerged and walked towards his car. She stepped out of the doorway and called his name, he ignored her and opened the car door. Ruth stepped forward taking a .38 calibre Smith & Wesson revolver from her handbag and fired five times at Blakely. She missed with the first shot and as Blakely ran she brought him down onto the pavement with the second shot and then calmly stood over him and fired three times into his body. The sixth bullet hit the pavement, rebounded and hit the hand of an innocent member of the public. Ruth turned to the petrified Gunnell and said 'Will you call the police please Clive'. She was arrested by an off-duty constable at the scene and taken to Hampstead Police Station where she seemed cool, calm and collected as she made a statement and was charged with murder.

Held in remand the psychiatrist and doctors who examined and questioned Ruth Ellis could find no evidence of insanity or diminished responsibility and even when in the witness box at her trial later she stated 'It is obvious that when I shot him I intended to kill him.'

On 20th June 1955 Ruth Ellis appeared at the Old Bailey charged with the murder of David Blakely and it took just 15 minutes for the jury to return a guilty verdict. The death sentence was passed and prisoner 9656 Ruth Ellis, age 28, was taken to the condemned cell at Holloway prison. She was hanged at 9am on Wednesday 13th July 1955 despite a 50,000 signature petition asking for clemency.

In 1969 Ruth Ellis's mother Berta Neilson, tried to commit suicide and was dragged from a gas filled room at her Hemel Hempstead flat. She never spoke coherently again having suffered damage to the brain due to lack of oxygen. Ruth Ellis's husband, George Ellis, hanged himself in 1958 and her son Andy, who was 10 at the time of her conviction and execution, suffered psychological damage and committed suicide in 1982. Ellis's daughter, Georgina, who was 3 at the time of her execution, was adopted after George Ellis hanged himself and died of cancer aged 50.

As was the custom at the time the body of Ruth Ellis was buried within the walls of Holloway Prison and when the prison was rebuilt in the early 70's all the executed women's bodies buried there were exhumed and reburied elsewhere. The body of Ruth Ellis lays in the graveyard at St Mary's Church in Amersham, Buckinghamshire. The headstone originally was inscribed 'Ruth Hornby 1926-1955'. The false name an effort to keep murder tourists away. That headstone was destroyed by her son, Andy, shortly before his suicide in 1982 and the grave is now overgrown.

MARIE MARGUERITE FAHMY

Born December 1890 – found not guilty by a jury on September 14th, 1923, died in Paris January 2nd 1971.

'Murder at the Savoy' Sounds like an Agatha Christie novel doesn't it? But this one isn't fiction.

French lady Marie-Marguerite Laurient 33, began an affair with 23 year old Egyptian Prince Ali Kamel Fahmy Bey in Paris in May 1922. Ali was not in fact a Prince but used the title to gain access to the elite social circles he enjoyed being part of. He was attached to the Egyptian Embassy in Paris and had a reputation for extravagance as well as it being rumoured that he was violent and bi-sexual. Laurient was a divorcee and had the reputation of being a 'gold- digger'. The pair went back to Cairo at the end of Ali's Paris posting and he suggested they live together as man and wife. Laurient refused insisting that they married which they did. What we now know as a *pre-nuptial agreement* was made with Laurient being allowed to wear western clothes and to be able to divorce Ali should she want to. In return she would adopt the Muslim faith which assured Ali of inheriting his family's wealth when his father died. He insisted the divorce clause be removed, which it was. The couple lived a life of wealth and extravagance in a large palace with servants, Rolls Royce cars, large boats and all the trimmings of the Egyptian elite.

But, within a short period of time the marriage was fraught with arguments and beatings of Laurient by

Ali who became an abusive person taking mistresses whilst having Laurient housebound and always accompanied whenever she went out. On July 10th 1923 they travelled to London and booked into and expensive suite at the Savoy Hotel in the Strand. That evening they quarrelled about a medical operation Laurient was due to have. She had seen a specialist about her external haemorrhoids and confided in the doctor these had been caused by her husband's 'unnatural intercourse' which he insisted on regularly. She wanted the operation done in Paris but Ali insisted it be done in London. The doctor had noted bruises on Laurient's face that had been ill-disguised with powder and make-up. The quarrel continued over the dinner table in the hotel dining room in front of other guests with both husband and wife threatening to smash a wine bottle on the other's head. It was all in French as Laurient spoke little English. They retired to their suite at 1.30am. Twenty minutes later a luggage porter was passing their door when Ali rushed out and seeing the man pointed to scratches on his face shouting 'Look what she has done to me!' The porter asked him to tone down a bit and collected the couple's small dog that had run out of the room and down the corridor and gave it to Ali before pulling the door shut. Almost immediately three pistol shots rang out from inside the room. The porter rushed back and on entering found Ali lying on the floor. The manager and hotel doctor were summoned and then an ambulance and the police. Ali was rushed to hospital but died that night.

Laurient was charged with Ali's murder and was sent for trial at the Central Criminal Court in London on September 10th, 1923. The trial created a stir with people queuing each day to get a seat in the small courtroom. It seemed an open and shut case but represented by two of England's most able lawyers, Sir Edward Marshall-Hall and Sir Henry Curtiss-Bennett, Laurient's defence was anything but open and shut. They portrayed Egyptian and Asian men in a very bad light and Ali as a violent man surrounded by an entourage of perverts, homosexuals and degenerates who vilified Laurient and made her life unbearable. On the night in question they said Ali had tried to kill Laurient by strangulation and supported that with medical evidence of bruising on Laurient's neck. When she had fought him off Ali fetched a pistol and came towards her gun in hand, a fight had ensued and Laurient had seized the gun and turned it on Ali as he grabbed her neck again shooting him three times in self defence. That defence scenario worked, the jury returned a verdict of not guilty of murder and not guilty of manslaughter. After the verdict and Laurient's release the prejudicial and racial undertones of the defence were called into question by the more moderate media. The defence had made many references to Ali being a wealthy 'oriental' playboy who, like others from that part of the world, preyed on western woman and had no decency values and treated them like sex slaves to be cast away when no longer wanted. The Egyptian ambassador called for an apology with this trial having consequences beyond the court room with political relations between the UK and Egypt going very cold for several months with Islamic and Muslim societies voicing their outrage at the lawyers' allegations.

If the prosecution had done their job properly they would have looked into Laurient's past and found out that she had been a teenage prostitute in Bordeaux and had an illegitimate daughter when just fifteen years old. In Paris she was known to like heroin and was well known as bi-sexual.

After the trial she went back to Paris and enjoyed being a minor celebrity for a few years, even appearing in low budget films. She sold her memoires to various English and French newspapers. She made an unsuccessful claim to Ali's fortune as he had not left a will and she even paid a family to 'borrow' their five year old son and present him as her and Ali's son to help claim the fortune. It didn't work. She was initially laughed at and then ignored by Parisian society and became a recluse. She never remarried and died on 2nd January 1971 in Paris.

SHEILA GARVIE

Born October 26th 1934 – sentenced to life in prison December 2nd 1968, released 1978.

Four in a bed then one was dead.

Maxwell Garvie owned West Cairnbeg Farm in Kincardinshire, Scotland and ran it with Sheila, his wife. The couple had married in 1955 and had three children. To their friends and relatives it was a marriage made in Heaven. But that it was definitely not. Both he and Sheila were enjoying the trappings of a wealthy life style in the 1960's, sex, drugs and rock n'roll. They had fast cars, continental holidays, a private plane and money. However, by this time friends of Sheila remember her complaining to them in private that her husband's sexual demands were 'abnormal'. By 1964 Maxwell became so obsessed with pornography and nudism that he enclosed part of the farm behind high thick hedges and founded a nudist camp. First it was just interested friends that were invited but it soon moved into sex orgies that Sheila refused to take part in at first but Maxwell was persuasive and insistent and soon she was involved and became quite enthusiastic according to others that took part. This kind of activity couldn't remain secret for long in the small community and pretty soon the Garvie farm was known locally as Kinky Cottage.

In 1967 22 year old Brian Tevendale began to help around the farm after visiting as a nudist with his sister Trudy Birse the wife of a local policeman whose marriage was on the rocks. Pretty soon Brian and Trudy had formed a regular sexual foursome with the Garvies. Sheila Garvie and Brian Tevendale were attracted to each other and this raised a problem for Maxwell who could see the relationship between the two getting stronger and the thought that Sheila might leave him for Tevendale filled his mind. He tried to end their relationship by banning Tevendale but Sheila wouldn't have it and things got heated between the three of them.

On 19th May 1968 Maxwell was reported missing to the police by his sister who had been unable to contact him since they last met on the 14th May at a Scottish Nationalist Party conference in Stonehaven. Maxwell, like his sister, was a very vocal promoter of Scottish Independence. His car was found on the runway at the Fordoun Flying Club where he kept his plane but there was no sign of him and a thorough search of local woods found nothing.

After a time Sheila Garvie admitted to her mother in confidence that Tevendale had told her he was responsible for Maxwell's disappearance and her husband was dead. The mother immediately broke that confidence and told the police of the conversation and both Sheila Garvie and Brian Tevendale were arrested on suspicion of committing murder. The next day, August 17th, Tevendale took the police to a large underground drain at Lauriston Castle near St. Cyrus and Maxwell's decomposing body was found. He had been beaten about the head and then shot in the head.

Tevendale implicated a friend, Alan Peters, in the killing. Garvie, Tevendale and Peters were all charged with Maxwell Garvie's murder. They all accused each other. Sheila Garvie claimed to have woken up in the middle of the night to find Tevendale and Peters in the house and her husband's murdered body on the kitchen floor. Tevendale said the killing was Sheila Garvie's idea and he was so infatuated with her he had agreed to do it.

At their trial at the Aberdeen High Court in November 1968 it also emerged that Maxwell Garvie and Trudy Birse were in a sexual relationship outside the foursome as she welcomed his 'abnormal' sexual demands. The crown prosecution claimed Sheila Garvie and Tevendale had plotted the murder between them so they could carry on their relationship and she would inherit the farm. On the night of the killing she had sex with her husband and when he was well asleep she had let Tevendale and Peters into the house and given Tevendale a .22 rifle and watched as he smashed Maxwell's skull with the butt and then shot him through a pillow to dull the noise of the shot so as not to wake the children. They then wrapped the corpse in a blanket and took it in the boot of Alan Peter's car to the drain at Lauriston Castle. Sheila had accompanied them in Maxwell's car which they dumped at the Flying Club air strip on the way back.

The jury found Alan Peters not guilty of murder but found Sheila Garvie and Brian Tevendale both guilty. The each received life sentences. Ten years later in 1978 both were paroled and released on licence. Tevendale became the landlord of a public house in Perthshire and died aged 58 in 2003. Alan Peters passed away in January 2007. Sheila Garvie married twice again. The first ended in divorce and in the second she was widowed. She led a simple life running a B&B in Stonehaven.

AUDREY HINGSTON

Born 1923 – guilty of manslaughter March 12, 2004, released October 5th 2004.

Audrey Hingston 81 of Underwood Road, Plymouth, Devon, stabbed her 85 year old husband, ex WW2 fighter pilot Eric, to death because he was bed ridden for many years and *'I'd had enough, I could not take any more of his illness and having to care for him.'*

On August 29th 2003 Audrey called an ambulance and police at 3.30am saying her husband had been attacked by burglars at their flat above a butcher's shop and had been stabbed in the chest and was lying on the floor. Eric was rushed to hospital but died on the way there. Police believed at the time that two burglars entered and left through Eric's bedroom window which was accessible from an adjoining flat roof. Audrey said she was woken by noises from Eric's bedroom and when she went in he was on the floor and the two burglars fled. But, things didn't look right. Drawers were scattered on the floor with the contents still inside, some of Audrey's jewellery was in a black bag by the window, why had the robbers left it? A ladder had been placed up to the flat roof which any person of normal height could have heaved themselves onto, it being just 5ft above the sloping back garden in parts. Audrey was able to give descriptions of the two burglars which fitted two local men who were arrested and released after their alibis were checked and confirmed. Both told police they knew the Hingstons and had done work on the property for them. Neither was a criminal or had a criminal record. Under questioning Audrey changed her story and said her husband had committed suicide after asking her to give him a 7inch kitchen knife, but the knife had been plunged up to the hilt into his chest entering his lung and his doctors claimed he was in no physical condition to do this. In the end Audrey was held in custody and admitted to her son a, detective on a different force, that she had killed Eric out of the frustration that had built up over years of caring for him 24 hours a day as his health deteriorated.

At Plymouth Crown Court on 11th March 2004 Audrey Hingston was found guilty of the manslaughter of Eric Hingston and was sentenced to two years in jail. The family were disappointed with the manslaughter verdict instead of one for murder and at such a lenient sentence being given. The police were also not happy and made a point of asking for the £160,000 spent on investigating Audrey's false claims to be reimbursed from any assets Audrey Hingston might have. The local MP asked the Attorney General to review the sentence but this was refused.

ELIZABETH MAUD JONES

Born 5th July1926 – sentenced to death January 22nd 1945, commuted to life in prison, released under license January 1954 age 27.

The English 'Bonny and Clyde'...well, sort of.

Elizabeth Maud Jones was born in Neath, South Wales. At 13 she ran away from home and was taken into care at an approved school after being deemed 'beyond control'. At just sixteen she married a soldier who was ten years older than her and left him on their wedding day after he lost his temper when she served him a cold dinner and had hit her. Jones was her own lady. A year later in January 1943 she was bored with Wales and made her way to the bright lights of London taking jobs as a barmaid, waitress, theatre usherette and stripper using a stage name of Georgina Grayson. In early 1944 she was out of work and surviving on the separation allowance her husband had been ordered by the family court to send her each week to live on.

On Tuesday 3rd October 1944 a friend of hers named Len Bexley, an out of work actor, introduced her to Karl Hulten who said he was an American Lieutenant. This was a lie as 22 year old Hulten was actually a private in the US military and had been absent without leave for six weeks from his unit stationed in England. Hulten and Jones took to each other immediately and agreed to meet later that day on a date for the late show at the local Cinema. Jones waited as arranged outside the cinema but there was no sign of Hulten. As a disappointed Jones walked off to go back to her lodgings a large two ton US army truck pulled up alongside her with Hulten waving from the driver's seat. She got in and they drove off for a night ride in the countryside. As they chatted she bemoaned the lack of excitement in her life which prompted Hulten to admit he was a deserter, had stolen the truck and had a pistol with him. At Reading they passed a girl on her bicycle and stopped a little further up the road so Hulten could jump out and push the girl off her bike to steal her purse. The girl made off and the couple drove back to London with Hulten dropping Jones off at around 5am. On the 5th October, two days later the pair went to the cinema in the evening and then set off for Reading again intending to rob a public house they had visited on the previous trip. However the publican had two large guard dogs and the plan was aborted. Back in London with their urge for excitement unfulfilled they decided to rob a taxi driver. They followed a cab from Marble Arch to Cricklewood and pulling the truck to a halt in front of the vehicle causing it to stop Hulten threatened the driver with the gun and robbed him before driving back towards Marble Arch. On the way back they picked up a young girl who was thumbing a lift to Paddington Station and offered to take her there. On the way Hulten faked a flat tyre and took an opportunity to knock her down with an iron bar and steal five shillings before leaving her unconscious body hidden off the road. They then went back to Jones lodgings and stayed until the afternoon arranging to meet again that evening.

Hulten arrived at around 11pm and they made a plan to rob another taxi driver. They hailed a Ford V8 private taxi in the Hammersmith road and the driver George Heath 34, agreed to take them to Chiswick Roundabout. When they arrived there Hulten shot Heath in the back. They pulled Heath, who was alive but paralysed, into the passenger seat and Hulten drove the taxi whilst Jones rifled Heath's pockets keeping money, a watch, and a cigarette case and throwing some letters, a cheque book and photos out of the window. A post-mortem on Heath at a later date estimated he had died from his wound within fifteen minutes from being shot. They dumped Heath's body near Staines in a roadside ditch and drove back to London. The left the car in a cinema carpark after wiping it clean of fingerprints had breakfast in a local cafe and went back to Jones room to sleep and plan their next move.

George Heath's body was found the next morning at about 9am by a fireman going home after his night shift. The letters, cheque book and photos had been found on the road earlier and collected by an apprentice on his way to work and handed into the police. Heath was quickly identified and listed as missing as was his car. The registration number was circulated within the police force.

Meanwhile Hulten sold Heath's watch and cigarette case to a jeweller for £6 which the pair spent that evening at the White City Dog track. They used Heath's car and left it parked behind an air raid shelter behind Fulham Palace Road early the next morning. It was discovered later that evening by a policeman on his beat and the detectives in charge of investigating Heath's murder visited the scene and noting how carefully the car had been parked well away from the public gaze they decided there was a good chance the killer(s) would return to use it again and so set up an observation post. At 9pm they saw Hulten arrive and they let him get into the car before pulling him out. A search revealed the Remington pistol used to kill Heath tucked under the driver's seat and he was arrested on suspicion of murder. At Hammersmith police station Hulten lied telling them he was 2nd Lieutenant Richard Allen of the 501 Parachute Regiment, US Army. The law at the time included a Visiting Forces Act which prohibited the police from taking any US Servicemen to trial in a British Court. The proceeding would be transferred to an American base for court martial or back to the US itself. An American officer was called in and he quickly established the true identity of Hulten and that he was a deserter. His alibi involved spending the time of the murder with Jones in her lodgings. Jones was brought in and gave a statement confessing to being at the scene of the murder and implicating Hulten as the killer. The American authorities had no wish to have anything to do with Hulten and certainly not be seen defending a murderer so they waved their legal rights and Hulten and Jones were sent for trial at the Old Bailey on Tuesday 16th January 1945. Both were found guilty of murder and sentenced to death. Both appealed and had their appeals turned down. Both were due to be hanged on the 8th March 1945. Two days before on the 6th Jones was reprieved. Hulten was not and was hanged on the appointed day at Pentonville Prison aged 23. Jones then 27, served 9 years before she was paroled under licence in January 1954. Her life from then on is unknown. A film *Chicago Joe and the Showgirl* was made in 1990 based on the story starring Emily Lloyd, Kiefer Sutherland and Patsy Kensit.

ETHEL LILLIE MAJOR née Brown.

Born 1892 – executed by hanging December 19th , 1934.

'The power of the pen.'

Ethel Brown was the only daughter of a Lincolnshire gamekeeper. She had three brothers and a good home life in a tied cottage on Sir Henry Hawley's estate where her father worked. She became a dress maker and fell pregnant at age 22 in 1914. There was a stigma to becoming an unmarried mother in those days and her parents decided to bring the child up in the family as Ethel's sister. In 1918 she married ex serviceman Arthur Major who was an unpleasant man with a drinking habit and a year later they had a son, Lawrence. In 1929 the family moved to Kirkby-on-Bain where Arthur drove a lorry for a gravel pit owner..

Ethel had grown into a nasty vindictive woman who was not liked at all in the neighbourhood and pretty soon rumours circulated about the 'younger sister' who often came to visit. The rumours reached Arthur who got the truth out of Ethel but she refused to name the father. Their relationship reached such a hate level that Ethel would not spend a night in the house with Arthur and would walk a mile to her father's house to sleep there. Ethel then accused Arthur of having a relationship with a neighbour and produced 'love letters' between the two. It later transpired she had written them herself although it was known locally that Arthur was indeed having the affair. Arthur retaliated and embarrassed Ethel by placing an advert in the local Horncastle News that he would not honour any debts incurred by his wife.

The embarrassment was more than Ethel, now 45, could take. She told his employer and the police that he was often drunk when driving his lorry. She tried to have the council house they lived in transferred to her name only so that she could evict him. In early 1934 Arthur began to have stomach pains telling his co-workers at the gravel pit that he was sure his wife was poisoning him. On 23rd May he took to his bed and the doctor was called. He found Arthur unable to control his body spasms or talk coherently. Ethel told the doctor that Arthur had had these fits before and they quickly wore off. The doctor concluded Arthur had mild epilepsy and prescribed a sedative. The next morning a weeping Ethel went to the doctors and told him Arthur had died over night. The doctor issued a death certificate listing heart failure as the cause. Ethel made plans for a quick funeral.

The very next day a note was popped through the door of the local police station, *"Sir, have you never heard of a wife poisoning her husband? You should look further into the death of Mr Major of Kirkby-on-Bain. Why did he complain that his food tasted nasty and throw it to a neighbour's dog which has soon died? Ask the undertaker why he stiffened so quickly? Why was he so jerky when dying? I and others have heard the wife threaten to poison him many times before. In the name of the law I beg you to analyse the contents of his stomach"* It was signed *"Fairplay"*

The police were sufficiently concerned that they had the coroner order a postponement of the funeral and sent Arthur's and the dead dog's bodies to a Home Office Pathologist at St Mary's Hospital Paddington for analysis. The results indicated that both had died from strychnine poisoning.

Ethel was taken in for questioning and said she suspected that some corn beef Arthur had bought cheaply was the culprit and she had nothing to do with preparing any of Arthur's meals and wouldn't buy corned beef herself. On her second interview she made the mistake of telling the officers, *"I have no idea how strychnine could have got into Arthur's food."* The lead officer, CI Hugh Young replied, *"We haven't mentioned strychnine, so how do you know that?"*

The house was thoroughly searched. No poison was found but CI Young decided to interview all the family about strychnine. Ethel's father admitted keeping some to kill vermin in his job. But knowing the power of the poison he kept it in a locked box and had the only key. There were originally two keys but one was lost years before. That 'lost' key was found on Ethel's key chain. It didn't fit any locks in the Major's house and she couldn't remember what it was for.

In November 1934 Ethel was sent for trial at Lincoln Assizes accused of the murder of Arthur Major. The jury returned a guilty verdict with a recommendation to the judge for mercy. This was ignored and she was sentenced to death. Ethel Major was hanged at Hull Prison on 19th December 1934 having been dragged screaming to the gallows. She was the first woman to be hanged at Hull Prison.

SUSAN HILDA MAY

Born 1945 – sentenced to life in prison May 5th 1993, released April 26, 2005.

Did she do it or did she not do it?

The small town of Royton sits between Oldham and Rochdale on the edge of Saddleworth Moor. The moor made famous by Ian Brady the serial killer as the place he buried the bodies. In 1993 Royton found itself on the front pages of the local and national newspapers after 89 year old local widow Hilda Marchbank was murdered. Mrs Marchbank who was almost completely blind had been battered and smothered to death. Her house was in such a mess with her possessions scattered on the floor that the police assumed she had been the victim of a burglary that went wrong. Eighteen days later they arrested Susan May, Mrs Marchbank's 48 year old niece.

Susan was born in Dogford Road, Royton the family house that she was still living in when arrested for Mrs Marchbank's murder all those years later. The family were fairly wealthy with her father owning several properties in the town that he collected rents from, often taking Susan with him. She had one sister called Ann. Her mother Dorothy had one older sister, Hilda, Susan's aunt who was married to the town's launderette owner Tom Marchbank. They had no children and doted on Susan and Ann as their own.

On leaving school Susan's parents set her up with her own hairdressing business. She married and the couple lived above the shop and when their third child arrived the flat was too small and her parents moved into one of the family's properties and Susan and her family moved into Dogford Road. In 1978 her father passed away and her mother, now with two hip replacements, moved back in with them. In the mid 1980s Susan and Terry separated and then divorced with Susan giving her ex husband half the value of the house to settle the divorce. She was financially helped in this by her mother. At this time her aunt, Hilda Marchbank, had been widowed and lived in Tandle Hill Road, a nice quiet tree lined street. She grew quite weak as age took its toll and lived mainly in the downstairs rooms of the house but was determined to stay there and not be moved into a care home. Susan agreed to help her as much as she could and with the care of her mother resting on her shoulders as well she gave up her school dinner lady job and became the carer to both.

On 11th March 1993 it was Susan's mother's birthday and Hilda was due to come for tea. During the morning her mother became ill and Susan went up to Hilda's in Tandle Hill Road to tell her not to come for tea. She took some soup and heated it up for the old lady before promising to come back the next morning as was the usual pattern of her daily visits. That evening Hilda phoned Susan asking where the house keys were. Susan thought this probably meant somebody had come to the door and Hilda had forgotten where she always kept the keys and couldn't open the door so she reminded her. Hilda rang again a little later asking the same question and Susan told her she would come up. Hilda told her not to bother the person at the door had now gone away. When the phone rang for the third time it was Christopher Ross, a man 16 years her junior who she had met eight years earlier when he and his wife were living next door and they have become lovers. He was now separated from his wife. He asked Susan to run him and a friend to the local public house if she had time. This she did stopping for ten minutes at Hilda's, going in through the back door and showing Hilda where the front door keys were always kept which Hilda had forgotten. She asked if there had been somebody at the front door but Hilda wasn't sure. That was the last time Susan saw her aunt alive.

The following morning Susan drove her daughter to Royton and bought a sandwich and cake for Hilda's lunch which she would drop off on the way home. She was surprised to find the curtains still drawn at 10am when she arrived at Hilda's and entered through the back door which was open. She found her aunt on her bed covered in blood. She ran to the next door neighbour and the police were called and set up a crime scene. Susan was allowed to go home to tell her mother but with police permission she told her that Hilda had died in her sleep. The truth would have been too much for her mother to bear. She didn't find out the truth until Susan's trial. The police exhausted their enquiries and questioning of all the known burglars in the area without getting a lead or suspect and turned to Susan because she had tried to keep Christopher Ross out of the picture and denied at first had any liaison. Their suspicion grew when Susan May's credit card debts of £7,000 surfaced, much of which had been used to buy Christopher Ross a car. A bereavement officer was assigned to the family and was surprised when Susan asked detailed questions about forensic methods including whether material from scratches on Hilda's face would be under the killer's fingernails. She would not know about the scratches as they would not have been visible under the blood on Hilda's face. Then Susan's fingerprint was found in a small blood stain on the wall of the room where Hilda was murdered by an officer two weeks after forensic officers had released the room back to the OIC (officer in charge) without mentioning it. The police decided they had the killer and arrested Susan May.

At her trial at Manchester Crown Court in May 1993 Susan denied making any remark to the bereavement officer about scratches and the notebook where the officer had logged the remark had gone missing. The police relied almost entirely on the relationship between Susan May and Christopher Ross as a motive for the crime. They put forward the notion that Susan killed her aunt Hilda for her money being scared that Ross would find a younger partner and end their relationship. But the defence pointed out that Susan had power of attorney over her aunt and could have taken money from Hilda's account at anytime if she had a mind to. She had also been made joint owner of three houses which were giving a good rental income into the account. She was also power of attorney over her mother's finances which gave her access to even more funds should she need it. The evidence crumbled with doubt being put on the fingerprint in the blood on the wall with the defence questioning why forensics didn't find it and the later test used to establish it was blood known as TAB using Tetra Aminobipheny was one that had been found erratic in the past presenting a high percentage of inaccurate results. The finger print only had a very few distinguishing marks when compared to Susan's finger print and not the required number of matching ridges. Neighbours came forward who had told the police of a red Ford Fiesta parked outside Hilda's house on the night of the murder with its engine running for 15 minutes. Another saw the car drive away with three men inside and gave good descriptions to the police. An anonymous phone call gave two names for the murder. Those names matched ones given six weeks before the murder by another caller about a burglary at another elderly person's home. The red Fiesta was traced to a known thief named Rawlinson, the car was sold two days after the murder of Hilda. Rawlinson was never treated as a serious suspect with his alibi that he stayed home all day and night with a friend and his girlfriend on the day of the murder being accepted without question by the police. The police had made up their mind that Susan May was the killer. They didn't pass on any information about the ref Fiesta or Rawlinson to Susan May's defence team.

Susan May was found guilty of the murder of Hilda Marchbank and sentenced to life in prison on May 5th 1993 with a 12 year minimum tariff. When in prison

Susan May never once deviated from her claim of innocence and even refused to take part in rehabilitation programmes aimed at murderers. Various reports have been commissioned about the case plus a Guardian Newspaper investigation. All have come to the conclusion that the police failed in their investigations and evidence of innocence was manipulated or disposed of and not used or passed to the defence. May's mother, Hilda Marchbank's sister, died a year after the conviction but like all the family she believed in Susan May's innocence. Susan May was released on April 26th 2005 being the first prisoner to be released straight away after serving a minimum tariff without licence terms whilst still denying the offence. She died in October 2013. Her family still fights to clear her name. Greater Manchester Police say it would not be appropriate to comment whilst appeals are ongoing. A review of the case by another force, Hampshire, concluded that 'anomalies' may well have led to Mrs May being wrongly convicted.'

JEMMA MITCHELL

1984 – sentenced to life in prison with a minimum tariff of 34 years.

Jemma Mitchell moved to the UK with her mother and sister from Australia when her parents' marriage broke down in 2004. She studied human sciences at King's College London which included dissecting the human body. She graduated with First Class Honours. She then returned for a short period to work in Australia before coming back to the UK in 2015 without a licence to practice here and lived with her now retired mother and sister in a family property in Willesden, N W London. The property had a value of £4m and had been in the family for several generations but was in a poor state of repair. Mitchell had several arguments with her sister and brother-in-law which resulted in a non-molestation order restricting her from contacting them in 2016. In 2020 she met Mee Kuen Chong at the church they both attended. Chong was a widow and had lived in London for 30years and suffered from paranoid schizophrenia and took medication for the illness. Both Mitchell and Chong were devout Christians and Chong was fooled by Mitchell into believing Mitchell was curing her illness with spiritual healing sessions. Chong's illness made her very gullible to Mitchell. Mitchell and her mother had planned to improve their house by adding a further floor and were scammed by a rogue builder who cheated them out of £230,000. Mitchell turned to Chong who she knew was very wealthy and persuaded her to loan £200,000 to complete the project. However Chong was legally advised it was not a secure investment with no guarantee of ever having her 'loan' repaid and so she backed out of the arrangement telling Mitchell to sell the house and enjoy the money.

On 11th June 2021 Mitchell travelled to Chong's house in Wembley, N London with a large suitcase and killed Chong before removing her head stuffing the body and head into the suitcase and taking it home with her later in the day. She also searched Chong's house taking documents from there and adding other documents she had stolen from a recently deceased neighbour's house. She then forged a will leaving Chong's £700,000 estate to herself. Chong was reported missing by her lodger and when the police questioned Mitchell she said she was under the impression Chong had gone to stay at friends on the coast as she had been feeling 'depressed'.

Chong's body in the suitcase was hidden in Mitchell's garden shed for a fortnight. She then used Chong's mobile phone that she had stolen to hire a car and on 26th June drove 320km to the Devon coast with the suitcase before taking Chong's body out of it and dumping it beside a footpath in Salcombe with the head hidden nearby. The body was found by holidaymakers the next day and the head recovered by cadaver dogs four days later. The body of 67 year old Chong was too decomposed to pinpoint the cause of death but it was noted at the post-mortem that her skull had been fractured. The police amassed enough evidence to prosecute Mitchell who was sent for trial at the Old Bailey on 22nd September 2022.

The court heard how Chong was killed after changing her mind about the £200,000 loan to Mitchell and shown CCTV footage of Mitchell arriving at Chong's house with the suitcase at 8.am on June 11th 2021 and leaving with it looking much heavier and bulky at 1.15pm plus a smaller bag of documents. CCTV showed her walking around London for two hours during which time the prosecution suggested she was looking for somewhere to dump the body. She then took a taxi home. The journey to Salcombe in the hire car was eventful as it had a flat tyre on the way and the AA repairman who attended recalled the suitcase and a distinctly musty smell. He found Mitchell to be a little confused and wondered why she would want to keep the flat tyre which he offered to dispose of as was the usual procedure. The forged will was presented in evidence as was the suitcase which had been found on the roof of a neighbour's garden shed. None of Chong's DNA was found inside the case but there was a bloodstained cloth in the pocket which had Chong's blood and DNA on it.

Mitchell did not give evidence in her defence but her lawyer made the point that the Mitchell house was valued at £4m and she had nearly £100,000 in a savings account so she did not have a financial motive to kill Chong.

The jury took seven hours to return a guilty verdict which had no visible effect on Mitchell. The sentencing by the judge would be the first of a convicted murderer to be televised live in England and Wales as well the first *woman* to have her sentencing live of television since a change in the law had now permitted this. Only the judge would be shown. Mitchell was sentenced to life in prison with a minimum tariff of 34 years which means she is not eligible for parole until July 2055.

SUSAN NEWELL

Born 1893 – October 10th 1923. Hanged,

Free Newspapers were not around in 1923 but she thought they should be!

Susan Newell was born in 1893 and was the last woman to be hanged in Scotland. In June 1923 she was living in a rented lodging in Newlands Street, Coatbridge, Glasgow, with her husband John and 8 year old daughter from a previous marriage, Janet McLeod. The marriage was a violent one with Susan having a bad temper and John being a drunkard that meant he never held a steady job. On the 19th June they had another row and the landlady had seen enough and gave them notice to quit. Susan was so incensed by this that she beat a drunken John about the head and kicked him when he fell on the floor. John thought he wasn't safe to stay with her and went to his sister's house nearby that night.

Next day on the 20th in the early evening a young newspaper seller John Johnson, 12, called and asked if Susan would like an evening paper. She invited him in and took a paper off him. She then refused to pay for it and when the boy took it back she lost control and strangled him. When her daughter came home the boy's body was on the floor. She helped her mother roll it inside the carpet and both went to bed.

In the morning they carried the carpet with the body inside down the stairs and put into an old pram with Janet sitting on top to steady it. Then they made their way to Glasgow centre to get rid of it. They even accepted a lift from a flat back lorry on the way and sat on the back with the pram. They left the lorry at Duke Street and as they lifted the bundle down from it John's foot slipped out of one end of the carpet roll and the top of his head could be seen at the other. They had refused help to unload the pram and the bundle from the driver who remained in his cab and saw nothing but local resident Mrs Helen Elliot was looking out of her first floor bedroom window in a house nearby and did notice it before Susan managed to cover up the head and foot. She told her sister what she had seen and they hurried out to follow the pram and asked the first man they saw to call the police. Luckily a policeman was close by and was soon up with them and together they saw Susan leave the rolled bundle with John's body in down an alleyway. Susan tried to flee but was caught as was Janet.

Susan Newell had already prepared her story and primed Janet to say the same. Both said her husband John had killed the news boy when drunk and that they had both tried to stop him. John was arrested and he and Susan were charged with murder.

The case came to trial in Glasgow on 18th September 1923 and John was released with the judge commenting to the police that he should never have been brought to trial as he had an alibi and several witnesses who were with him that evening in another town gave evidence on his behalf. Then Janet, who hadn't been charged, broke down in the witness box and told the court the truth about finding the body in the flat and helping her mother tie it inside a carpet and then her mother telling her the story to tell the police about her step-father killing the news boy. Susan carried on denying she had killed John Johnson and kept to the story that it was her husband who had strangled him. The jury did not believe her and found her guilty of the boy's murder with a recommendation for mercy. The judge sentenced her to death and ordered her to be taken to Glasgow prison and examined by psychiatrists. This was done and their unanimous conclusion was that she was perfectly sane. No woman had been hanged in Scotland for fifty years but the law was the law and no reprieve was forthcoming from the Scottish Secretary of State and Susan Newell was hanged on October 10th 1923 in Duke Street prison. She was the very last woman to be hanged in Scotland.

One interesting aside to the case is that Susan Newell refused to have the white hood over her head whilst standing on the gallows and John Ellis, the executioner had to stand face to face with her as he slipped on and adjusted the noose. He would usually slip the hood on before standing in front of the condemned person to adjust the noose with no eye contact. He said afterwards that it had no effect on him but within eight weeks he resigned after 23 years doing the job. Then, apparently suffering from depression he tried to commit suicide by shooting himself. He survived and appeared on stage taking 'hangman' parts in plays and also gave talks on his experiences in that job. But in September 1932 he cut his own throat.

BEATRICE ANNIE PACE

Born 1892 – July 6th 1928 convicted and named by the jury for murdering her husband with arsenic but public sentiment had her acquitted.

Just the name of the place and the farm reads like a dark Dickens novel.

Beatrice Pace had been married to Harry Pace for eighteen years and they eked out a meagre living from a few sheep on his land at Starve Acre farm, Bleak Moor, Fetterhill in the Forest of Dean, Gloucestershire supplemented by his pay for irregular work as a stone quarryman. They had five children to support.

On January 10th 1928, after a long illness Harry Pace died. The death certificate gave 'natural causes' but Beatrice and the older children were not happy with that as Harry was a fit man before the illness which the doctor could not name. A police investigation followed with a post mortem at the coroner's request who postponed the funeral. Forensic analysis found that Harry had died from arsenic poisoning of three times the lethal dosage and his family's concerns were justified.

Harry's illness had started in July 1927after he and Beatrice had done the annual sheep dipping where the animals were dipped in an arsenic based solution to kill any parasites in their wool. Harry had been taken into hospital when the illness worsened but made little progress and returned home for Beatrice to care for him and seemed to make some improvement at first but then lapsed back and after Xmas he died.

Rumours in the Forest of Dean spread, mainly put about by Beatrice's in-laws who accused her of adultery and neglecting his nursing needs. On the other side locals talked of his known violent temper and of regularly seeing the bruises on Beatrice and the children and of how he would fall into deep depression at times.

The coroner's jury reached a verdict that Harry had been 'poisoned by person or persons unknown' and recommended further investigation, But the coroner cited the law that said the jury must name the person responsible. They named Beatrice Pace as the murderer and she was remanded in prison.

There was public outrage at this as the media had published the facts of Harry Pace's violence towards his family and how Beatrice had endured eighteen years of it to protect her children, of how he had locked them out of the house in the cold winter, of how he killing their dog, of how he brought prostitutes to the house for sex, and of how another five children had died in their early years of 'natural causes'. Public money was raised to provide Beatrice with a top defence team who tore into the prosecution and their 'hearsay' witnesses at the Gloucester Trial on July 6th 1928 asserting that they had failed totally to make a case. The judge agreed and instructed the jury to find Beatrice Pace not guilty. A crowd of 600 gathered outside the court and cheered the verdict and the road from Gloucester to Coleford, near Fetter Hill was lined with cheering people as Beatrice went home, hopefully to a better life.

MARIA PEARSON

Born 12th March 1956 – sentenced to life in prison with an 11 year tariff in 1987. She remains inside.

Maria Pearson is known as 'The UK's Forgotten Inmate'. She is notable for being the UK's longest serving female prisoner.

Pearson, from Hartlepool, had been married twice and had two children before she bigamously married Malcolm Pearson in February 1986 after they had a child together. Shortly after the wedding their relationship began to fail with violent fights between the pair a regular occurrence and after just one month of marriage they separated.

Malcolm started a new relationship with 23 year old Janet Newton and Maria, now 31, became overwhelmed with jealousy and hatred towards Janet to the extent of stalking her through the streets of Hartlepool and shouting abuse at her in public. She also sent Janet's mother hate mail.

Just two days after Malcolm and Janet celebrated becoming engaged Maria set upon Janet in Grange Road and stabbed her 17 times including twice through the heart, killing her. Police and ambulance attending the horrific scene thought at first that it had been a car accident due to the ferocity of the attack.

In early 1987 Pearson was sentenced to life in prison with a minimum tariff of 11 years. Twenty five years after that 11 year tariff expired she is still in prison. As at this time she has been denied parole nine times. The reasons being that she has refused to take part in any rehabilitation courses and when sent to open prisons has had to be returned to a closed one after poor behaviour in public including assault and intimidation. She has refused to admit her guilt still insisting, as she did at her trial, that yes, she did kill Janet Newton but '*as an act of self-defence after provocation*'. Her appeal to the Criminal Cases Review Commission has been turned down. Her latest parole rejection was February 2023 with a strong protest at any release from Janet Newton's family saying she should never be released as you cannot 'rehabilitate psychos'. At that time she has served just one year less than Myra Hindley the Moors Serial Murderer who was never released from prison and died inside in 2002.

ANNE PERRY
(born Juliet Marion Hulme)

Born 28th October 1938 – died 10th April 2023

Anne Perry was a best-selling British author best known for the *Thomas and Charlotte Pitt* and the *William Monk* series of historical detective fiction books.

Perry was the daughter of Physicist Henry Rainsford Hulme and after being diagnosed with tuberculosis as a child she was sent first to the Caribbean and then to New Zealand to benefit from the warmer climates. Her father took a position in New Zealand and the family settled there in Christchurch.

On June 22nd 1954 aged just 15 and together with her best friend, Pauline Parker, they murdered Pauline's mother in Victoria Park, Christchurch by battering her over twenty times with a brick hidden in a stocking. These events formed the basis for the film Heavenly Creatures released in 1994 with Kate Winslet playing Hulme who had reverted to using her father's name, Perry.

They stood trial at Christchurch for murder and were found guilty but were too young to be given the death penalty, which was still available under New Zealand law at that time, and so both were detained 'at Her Majesty's Pleasure'. They were released separately five years later. It is understood the two never met or corresponded after their release.

After being released in 1959 Hulme returned to England and after a period of living here and in the USA she settled in the Scottish village of Portmahomack with her mother. Here she took the name Anne Perry using her stepfather's name and began a writing career. Her first novel The Cater Street Hangman was published in 1979 under his name. She had success as an author with financial and critical success in the historical murder mystery genre with her series featuring *Thomas and Charlotte Pitt* and private investigator *William Monk* being her best sellers.

Media journalists unearthed her past as a murderer and revealed her true identity in 1994 after the film Heavenly Creatures came out.

She said: *It seemed so unfair. Everything I had worked to achieve as a decent member of society was threatened. And once again my life was being interpreted by someone else. It had happened in court when, as a minor, I wasn't allowed to speak and I heard all these lies being told. And now there was a film, but nobody had bothered to talk to me. I knew nothing about it until the day before its release. All I could think of was that my life would fall apart and that it might kill my mother.*

She continued writing saying how she was surprised and grateful to her many friends and readers who had stuck by her. Her books won numerous awards and sales exceeded 10 million by 2015.

In 2017 she moved to Los Angeles to help in the promotion of several films and TV series based on her books. In December 2022 she had a heart attack and on 10th April 2023 aged 84 she died.

FLORENCE RANSOM

Born 1906 – sentenced to death 6th November 1940. Later adjudged to be insane and transferred to Broadmoor.

Murders by women using a gun are exceedingly rare which is why this one got in the list.

Married couple Laurence and Dorothy Fisher lived in Twickenham, a London Suburb. When their marriage broke down they separated and went their own ways. Laurence fell for Florence Ransom, a wealthy young widow who owned a farm in Oxfordshire. The two would meet at weekends at a cottage Laurence owned at Matfield near Tonbridge in Kent. When WW2 broke out Laurence handed over the cottage to his ex wife Dorothy and her daughter aged 19 whilst he moved into the farm with Florence. It seems the Fisher's divorce had been quite friendly and they still had a good relationship. In fact Laurence would check on the mother and daughter at the cottage after air raids and provided financial help so that a housekeeper could be employed.

In the background Florence Ransom was seething with jealousy at his continued relationship with his ex and on July 8th 1940 she borrowed a rifle from her brother saying she was going rabbit shooting and took the train to London. That much we know, her movements after that are very hazy. A railway porter at Tonbridge *thought* he saw her leaving the station but couldn't be sure. A bus could be taken from Tonbridge to Matfield. A taxi driver *thought* he saw her board the London train from Tonbridge later that afternoon but he also couldn't be sure.

The only sure thing was that sometime during that afternoon Mrs Fisher and her daughter had been shot in the back and killed and their housekeeper had half her head blown off whilst standing in or running through a nearby wooded area. The house had been ransacked but nothing taken. The assailant had managed to re-load the rifle at least twice after the first shot as it took just one bullet into the breach at a time. Why two of the victims had not been able to run away after the first shot was baffling.

The main evidence that Florence Ransom was the killer was a woman's white leather glove dropped on the cottage floor. The glove belonged to Florence Ransom.

Then three reliable witnesses came forward. William Smith a young charcoal burner said he cycled past the cottage at about 1.45pm and saw two bicycles in the drive, on his return at 3.30pm he saw a lady's cycle on the ground about 50 metres from the cottage. Then further on down the road he saw a woman carrying a long brown paper parcel walking towards Tonbridge. He picked out that woman as Florence Ransom in an identity parade. Further down the road to Tonbridge he stopped to talk to John Elphick and the pair saw Florence Ransom pass them walking very fast towards Tonbridge. Albert Skilton lived a quarter of a mile down the road from the cottage and at about 12.45pm on the day of the murders he was standing in his front and saw Dorothy Fisher go by on a bike together with a lady who walking. He identified Florence Ransom from a photograph. William Edgar Playfoot was loading his baker's van outside his shop on the Matfield to Tonbridge Road when a lady he later identified as Florence Ransom asked for a lift to Tonbridge if he was going that way as she had a train to catch. He was so he drove her there in silence and dropped her off.

She went to trial at the Old Bailey in November 1940 and offered a defence that she did not remember a single thing. Her memory of that day was a complete blank. The court heard that she had a record of mental instability and had been a voluntary patient in several mental institutions at various times. However, her defence had not brought any medical evidence of this and so after a guilty verdict from the jury the judge had no alternative but to give the death sentence. She was then examined by psychiatrists, pronounced insane and sent to Broadmoor with the sentence changed to life in prison.

What happened to Laurence Fisher is not recorded.

FREDA PHYLIS RUMBOLD

Born 1913 – sentenced to death November 22nd 1956, commuted to life in prison.

Alfred and Freda Rumbold were married in 1933. Over the years Alfred had built up a small but prosperous timber business in Bristol and the couple had no money worries. The marriage was not a happy one and Freda would receive beatings from Alfred accompanied by sexual demands. Twice she had reported him to the police for violence and he had been given warnings. Freda, now 44, devised a plan to rid herself of Alfred. She bought a gun from a shop in Yeovil and ammunition for it from Taunton telling her friends that it was a present for a friend who was going shooting in Scotland.

On Tuesday August 21st 1956 they entertained friends at their home and those present didn't sense anything out of the ordinary between the couple. The next evening they spent time together at the local public house before going home at about 10.30pm.

They slept in separate rooms as Freda was not happy with Alfred's increasing demands for what she said later to the police 'were unhealthy sex acts'. That night once Alfred was asleep Freda entered his room with the gun and shot him in the head from close range. She calmly reloaded and fired a second shot that missed and buried itself in the wall. Freda then calmly went to her own room and slept. The next morning she soaked a towel in disinfectant and stuffed it between the bottom of Alfred's bedroom door and the floor and hid the gun between mattresses in a spare bedroom. She then went to Alfred's business and told the employees he had gone on a business trip and didn't know how long it would take and had left her in charge. Back home she wrote a letter to her mother saying they had split up and Alfred had left but had generously given her his business, the house and bank account. She even sent a copy of a typewritten authorisation confirming this with his forged signature at the bottom.

Freda then carried on as if nothing had happened but by Saturday the smell from Alfred's decomposing body was beginning to permeate through the house. Freda wrote a notice 'Please Do Not Enter' and pinned it to Alfred's bedroom door.

Realising she had to do something Freda went to her sister's house and told her that she and Alfred had an argument and he had threatened to shoot her. They had struggled, the gun went off and Alfred was dead. Her sister informed the police who secured the house and took Freda into custody.

The police did not believe her story and Freda was sent for trial at Bristol in November 1956 on the charge of murdering Alfred Rumbold.

Freda said that on the night Alfred was killed he had been in bed and she was downstairs doing housework when she heard a shot. She ran upstairs and found Alfred sitting in bed with the gun in his hand pointed at his head. She made a lunge for the gun but it went off shooting Alfred in the head. She was afraid to call the police as she knew her record of reporting him twice for violence in the past might put her under suspicion. She admitted buying the gun and ammunition but said it was for self-protection. The gun had been recovered from between the two mattresses but had no fingerprints on it, she had wiped it clean. The prosecution called attention to the fact there were two bullets and Alfred Rumbold would hardly have missed his own head if the bullet in the wall was the first shot. The defence claim of it being an accident didn't convince the jury who had heard from witnesses of the Rumbold's unhappy marriage and been told the facts that Freda had bought the gun, bought the ammunition, wiped it clean after the shooting and then had hidden it and forged a letter to her mother. They also heard from Alfred Rumbold's bank that she had tried to take a considerable sum of money out of his business account two days after the murder but the signature was questioned.

Freda Rumbold was found guilty of murder and sentenced to death which was later commuted to life in prison by the appeal court who took into consideration findings from psychiatrists that the beatings and mental harassment she had suffered from her husband would have affected her mind.

LAKHVIR KAUR SINGH

Born 1969 – February 11th 2010 sentenced to life in prison with a minimum tariff of 23 years.

This case is unusual because of the killer's weapon, an ancient poison named aconitine that she travelled to India to buy.

On 27th January 2009 in the predominantly Asian area of Southall, West London, Lakhvinder Cheema, 39, was murdered by his former lover Lakhvir Kaur Singh 45. Singh had used a poison called aconitine that is derived from the Aconitum Ferox plant which she had travelled to India to buy.

Singh and Cheema had a 16 year affair after his first marriage had broken down. Cheema was married with three children.

Singh told Cheema he was ending their affair in November 2008 as he had met a younger woman named Choongh, 21, to whom he was getting engaged to. Singh previously told Cheema of his affair with the younger woman and she had threatened to burn down his house with the pair of them in it.

Red flags were waving in December 2008 when Cheema was hospitalised after eating a meal prepared by Singh during which she implored him to cancel his engagement and continue their affair. He refused. Two weeks later Singh took a quick four day trip to India and brought back the aconite poison. On 27th January she went into Cheema's house that she still had the keys to and put aconite into a dish of left-over curry she found in his fridge knowing that he would heat it up and eat it. The plan worked with both Cheema and his fiancé Choongh eating the curry as they discussed their wedding plans at his home in Princes Road, Feltham, West London with Cheema even having a second helping. Soon after the meal both began to feel very ill and vomit uncontrollably. Cheema went blind and lost the use of his limbs, and his sister who was visiting at the time, but not eaten the meal, managed to get him and Choongh to hospital where Cheema died within an hour.

Victims of aconite poisoning suffer severe vomiting, paralysis and have the sensation of ants crawling all over their skin. Their organs cease to work and they die from self induced asphyxiation and horribly remain conscious throughout. Murder by aconite is very rare and the last known case brought to court in the UK was 1882.

Choongh survived after being placed on a medically induced coma and having her stomach pumped. Cheema had told his sister that he thought Singh had poisoned the curry before he had lapsed into unconsciousness and she told the police.

Two lodgers in Cheema's house gave police a statement that they had seen Singh go to Cheema's fridge and remove the curry although they had not seen her add anything to it. Singh's home was searched and a small plastic bag of brown powder was found in her coat pocket which she said was to be mixed with water and made into an ointment for a rash on her neck. Forensic analysis found it to be aconite. Aconite was also found in the remains of the curry and in both Cheema and Choongh's stomach contents.

At the Old Bailey on 10th February 2010 Singh was found guilty of the murder of Lakhvinder Cheema and grievous bodily harm against his fiancé. Singh received a life sentence with a minimum tariff of 23 years. The prosecution had sought a tariff of 30 years due to the obvious premeditation of the crime.

EMILY SWANN

Born 1861 - December 29th 1903. Hanged.

This case just scrapes into the time frame of the book but is interesting as it resulted in a double hanging.

Emily Swann, 42, had eleven children. She was described as a stumpy little woman of barely 4ft 10in tall. She was married to William Swan who was a skilled glass blower and they lived in Wombwell, Yorkshire where they had taken in a lodger, John Gallagher, a 30 year old miner. Times were hard in the early 1900s and the rent paid to them by Gallagher came in useful with eleven mouths to feed.

The relationship between Emily and William Swan was peppered with violence and the neighbours had common knowledge that he beat her up quite often. Domestic violence was common at the time and attitudes to a man beating his wife were very different from today. Attitudes to extra marital affairs were different too so when Emily started one with the lodger John Gallagher the quarrels increased and Gallagher decided it best to move elsewhere where he and Emily could continue their meetings in peace and so he moved to Bradford.

On the 6th June 1906 Emily turned up to meet John at a neighbour's house in Wombwell with two black eyes and a bruised face. John was incensed and rushed to find and confront William shouting, 'I'll coffin him so I will'.

The sounds of a fight came from inside the Swann's house and Emily went inside and could be heard egging Gallagher on telling him to, 'Give it to him Johnny.'

After a while all went quiet and Emily and John emerged from the house joking that 'the bastard is gone.' A neighbour ventured inside and found William lying on the floor, dead.

The police were summoned and arrested Emily but John had fled and gone on the run before being found and arrested at a relative's house in Middlesborough two months later.

They were both sent for trial in October 1903 at Leeds Assizes with both pleading that the death was an accident and John was only going to teach William a lesson. But the remarks about 'putting him in a coffin' that were heard by neighbours were told to the jury with the prosecutor insisting William Swan's death was therefore a pre-meditated murder.

Both were found guilty and sentenced to death and remanded to Armley prison in Leeds where their defence lawyers put in appeals which were both turned down.

On December 29th Emily Swan was taken into the gallows room at Armley jail where John Gallagher had already been brought and had a white hood placed over his head so he couldn't see Emily arrive. But she could see him and said 'Good morning John' to which he replied, 'Good morning my love'. As they stood side by side on the gallows with nooses around their necks Emily said, 'Good-bye John, God bless you,' he replied,

'I'll see you soon,' and the traps were both opened simultaneously.

Double hangings were in future to be carried out simultaneously but at different prisons so no words could be exchanged between the prisoners.

DENA THOMPSON

Born 1960 – sentenced to life in prison 2003 with 16 year tariff. Released on parole in June 2022.

Dena Thompson is known as The Black Widow. She is a confidence trickster, murderer and bigamist suspected of having murdered a second person.

Thompson was born Dena Holmes in Hendon, North London in1960 and was a cashier in a Building Society. She met Lee Wyatt in 1982 and they married two years later in 1984. Wyatt was mentally unstable with a fantasist view of life and was convinced by Thompson that he had £50m in a secret account from a child's toy he had patented and the mafia were after his money. So convincing was she that Wyatt left home and lived homeless for years to escape the mafia. Thompson stole £23,000 from the Building Society where she was working and blamed it on Wyatt. It was obvious he couldn't do such a crime and in 1955 she was jailed for 18 months. With the help of Social Service they divorced in 1997.

During the marriage to Wyatt, Thompson bigamously married Julian Webb in 1991 and murdered him by poisoning a curry he ate in June 1994 with an overdose of anti-depressants and ground up aspirin tablets. The inquest on Webb's death recorded an open verdict and the speed at which she tried unsuccessfully to have his body cremated the day after the inquest really should have alerted the coroner to something not being right. But it didn't. That same day she tried to collect £35,000 which would have been released from his pension plan on his death to his next of kin, but Webb's mother stopped that as she was able to prove the marriage was bigamous as Holmes was at that time still married to Lee Wyatt.

After the divorce from Wyatt in 1997 Holmes married Richard Thompson the very next year. They lived in Rustington, Sussex. On January 1st 2000 she suggested a sex game where she blindfolded him and tied him up with a rope. He agreed and once he was blindfolded and tied up she attacked him with a baseball bat and knife. Miraculously he managed to escape the rope and she confessed it was because she had spent all his money and didn't know how to tell him and was going to kill him and tell the police it was a robbery by others. For some reason Thompson did not call the police. The next day an estate agent turned up at the house where Thompson was recovering from the attack and told him that Dena had put the house on the market. The estate agent had been told Thompson, part owner of the property, was in the USA and would sign the sale papers on his return. It later emerged that Dena had planned to kill Thompson and sell the house whilst telling people he was on a pre-booked business trip to America. No one would be suspicious at his disappearance for some time as he was actually due to go to America and his friends were aware of this. Once the house was sold and she had the money she would tell people she was joining him and they were going to live in America. She would then disappear with the money. What she planned to do with Thompson's body is not known.

Thompson now called in the police and Dena was arrested. The police interviews with her former partners uncovered that she had stolen money from all of them and emptied their bank accounts after persuading them to have a joint account. Thompson's bank account had also been emptied.

She denied trying to murder Thompson saying he had attacked her after finding his money had gone and she had retaliated in self-defence.

She was acquitted of attempted murder and convicted of 15 counts of deception and was given 3 years and 9 months.

The police officers investigating the case became very suspicious of Dena over the death of her second husband, Julian Webb, 6 years before. They were granted an exhumation order and the body was taken for analysis in October 2001.

The remains of the anti-depressants and aspirin were found to be present in quantities that were high enough to kill Webb. Dena Thompson was sent for trial at the Old Bailey in 2003, found guilty of his murder and sentenced to life in prison. The press dubbed her The Black Widow after the black widow spider that kills its male partner after mating with them.

On 23rd May 2022 it was announced Dena Thompson had been granted early release on parole and would be released in June. The parole report stated that they were satisfied with her progress in prison and that she was suitable for release.

Several documentaries have been made featuring Dena Thompson and the case.

EDITH JESSIE THOMPSON

Born December 25th 1893 – hanged at Pentonville Prison January 9th 1923.

See Frederick Bywaters in Volume 1 of the UK KILLERS series.Edith Jessie Thompson 25th December 1893 - 9th January 1923 and her lover Frederick Edward Francis Bywaters were a British couple who were hanged for murdering Thompson's husband Percy. The case became a major talking point creating press headlines for some while.

Thompson born Edith Graydon at 97 Norfolk Road, Dalston, London was one of five children of William Graydon, a clerk and Ethel Jessie Liles, the daughter of a police constable.

Thompson was a talented child excelling at her school work with a natural ability in mathematics. She left school to work as a bookkeeper in a London fashion company and worked her way up in that company to become their chief fabric buyer which necessitated regular trips to Paris. She married businessman Percy Thompson in 1916 and they bought a large house in Ilford, Essex and settled into a comfortable life style.

They met Freddy Bywaters, 20, in 1920 and Edith, then 28, was attracted to him by his stories of his travels around the world as a merchant seaman. He was the opposite of her down to earth husband and the regular life they led. The three became good friends and when Freddy returned from one of his long cruises he was invited to lodge with them. After a while Percy became aware of his wife and Bywater's having an affair and ordered Bywaters to leave the house. This he did and signed onto another voyage during which time Edith wrote to him a lot describing how Percy had taken to beating her. This was a total lie. She kept up the accusations of mistreatment when Freddy returned from sea and they continued their affair in secret.

On October 3rd 1922 the Thompsons were returning home from a night at the theatre in London when a man jumped from the bushes near their home and attacked Percy violently by stabbing him before running off. Percy died at the scene and Edith told the police that she didn't recognise the attacker but a neighbour had recognised him as the Thompson's old lodger and that it was Freddy Bywaters. Edith then confided in the officers about her romantic involvement with Bywaters falsely assuming she would be a witness and not charged as an accomplice to murder.

Bywaters was arrested and so was Edith after finding more than sixty love letters at his lodgings from her with some expressing her wish for Percy to be killed. Under English law if two people with to achieve the death of a third person and one of them acts to achieve this end, then both are guilty of the murder as the act had been the expressed intention of both. Both Edith and Freddy were charged with Percy's murder.

At the Old Bailey trial in 1922 Bywaters admitted the killing and maintained he had acted alone without Edith's knowledge. The love letters were produced for the jury to read by the prosecution. In them she expressed her wish to be free of Percy and how she had laced his food with ground glass and poison several times. This had failed and she had asked Freddy to 'do something desperate'. She said she had no idea what she had meant by this and became very arrogant and dismissing toward the court and jury.

On December 11th 1922 both she and Bywaters were found guilty of murder and sentenced to death. Edith screamed her innocence and Freddy shouted at the jury. The public had been following the case on the front pages of the press and changed from hating Edith to thinking of her as a stupid, foolish woman befuddled by love, and a million signature petition against the death sentence was handed into the Home Office. To hang a woman was considered abhorrent and no woman had been hung in the UK since 1907. However the Home Secretary refused to offer a reprieve.

Confined to her cell, Edith lost her mind and spent the last days screaming and crying before having to be carried to the scaffold on January 9th 1923 by the executioner, John Ellis, his assistant and two warders where she then had to be held upright as the noose was fitted. Not a nice picture to imagine. She was hanged at 9am in Holloway Prison at exactly the same time as Freddy Bywaters was hung at Pentonville Prison just half a mile away. Both bodies were buried within the walls of those two prisons. Edith's was re-buried in Brookwood cemetery, Surrey in 1970 when Holloway prison was rebuiltThe Home Office files on the case and the court transcripts were closed for 100 years and have just recently become available. They make interesting reading for students of British law and court procedure but lay outside the parameters of this book.

LORRAINE THORPE

Born 1994 – ordered to be detained for a minimum 14 years on September 7th, 2010.

Lorraine Thorpe, at the time of compiling this book, is Britain's youngest female double murderer, being just 15 years old at the time of the killings.

She was born in Ipswich, Suffolk and lived in a poor, run down district moving around with her father, Desmond Thorpe, an alcoholic, from squalid flat to squalid flat and sometimes even in tents in the open community areas with a group of older alcoholics who were violent and lived mainly by theft. She came to the notice of the Ipswich Social Services at an early age but they repeatedly lost contact with her as she moved around.

The leader of the group Thorpe moved around with was Paul Clarke, 41, a very violent man who struck up an abusive relationship with Thorpe, 15. In August 2009 the pair had an argument with Rosalyn Hunt, another member of their circle of drinkers. They rowed over a dog and the pair called at Hunt's flat in Victoria Street, Ipswich and beat, kicked and punched her to death after three days of torturing her with cheese grater, dog chain and salt they rubbed into her wounds.

On August 9th a neighbour called the police to Hunt's flat after being concerned for her safety having not seen any movement at the flat for some time. Hunt's body was found and a murder hunt started. To cover their tracks Thorpe and Clarke decided to kill Thorpe's father who was disabled and in a wheel chair with Thorpe as his carer. They were afraid he would implicate them in the murder whilst he was in one of his drunken states. Thorpe smothered her father with a cushion and beat and kicked his dead body on the floor just to make sure. She kicked him so viciously that pathologists later found imprints of her boot on his head.

On the 10th August 2009 they rang the police anonymously and said the body of a man was lying in Limerick Close. The police linked the two murders and arrested both Thorpe and Clarke.

At their trial a year later at the Old Bailey on August 4th 2010 Clarke was deemed to have been the instigator of the killings and was sentenced to life with a minimum term of 27 years and Thorpe's sentencing was delayed until September when she too was sentenced to life in prison with a minimum tariff of 14 years.

Both had appeals against their conviction for the murder of Desmond Thorpe turned down by the Court of Appeal who said they were convinced the convictions were safe. Neither of them appealed against the Rosalyn Hunt convictions for murder.

In September Clarke committed suicide in HM Prison Whitemoor.

As far as we know Thorpe is in HM Prison Foston Hall in Derbyshire, a closed prison for female offenders. She is due to have her first parole hearing in 2023.

The case has been the subject of many documentaries. An investigation into Ipswich Social

Services handling of Lorraine Thorpe has not been published in the public domain.

DOROTHEA NANCY WADDINGHAM

Born 1899 – April 16th 1938. Hanged

Dorothea was born at Hucknall, Nottingham and worked in factories before taking a post at the Burton on Trent Workhouse Infirmary in Staffordshire. She gained basic medical knowledge there and began passing herself off as a nurse. She had three children with husband Thomas Leech who she married in 1925 just eight years before he died of cancer.

Dorothea then reverted to her maiden name and started a relationship with her lodger Ronald Sullivan, six years older than her. Together they opened a nursing home at 32 Devon Drive, Nottingham which was approved by the authorities who considered Dorothea to be a competent nurse and carer.

On 12th January 1935 the County Nursing Association asked them to care for two patients for £1.50 a week payment. The patients were Louisa Baguley an 89 year old widow and her 50 year old daughter Ada. Ada was disabled and used a wheelchair and her elderly mother could no longer look after her.

On 4th May 1935 Ada Baguley contacted her solicitor and asked him to come and change her will. All her £1,600 of savings would go to Dorothea and Ronald on condition they looked after her mother Louisa and herself for the rest of their lives. There were rumours that Dorothea had threatened to send the pair of them to the workhouse as the £1.50 a week was not enough to keep them.

On 12th May 1935 Louisa Baguley died. The death of a near ninety year old did not raise any suspicions and the doctor issued a death certificate allowing her burial.

Ada continued to live at the 'Nursing Home' until on the 11th September she suddenly died although visitors to her the previous day had found her cheerful, in good spirits and quite well. Dr Mansfield, who had attended both Louisa and Ada was summoned and put the cause of Ada's death down to a cerebral haemorrhage. Dorothea produced a letter written by Ada on 29th August asking to be cremated and not buried. Dr Mansfield issued both a death certificate and a permit for cremation. Fortunately, Nottingham's Medical Officer for Health, DR Cyril Banks, had to approve the cremation and was suspicious of the letter which had been written by Ronald Sullivan and signed by Ada and had the sentence, *'my last wish is that my relatives should not be informed of my death'* added in different ink and squashed in at the end. Dr Banks ordered a post mortem that revealed Ada had been poisoned with morphine. The police were brought in and had Louisa's body exhumed and morphine was found in her remains as well.

Dorothea and Ronald were arrested, charged with the murders of Ada and Louisa Baguley and remanded in prison.

On 24th February 1936 they appeared at Nottingham Assizes. The judge dismissed the charges against Ronald and discharged him on the second day of the trial due to lack of any real evidence. This was just as well as the couple had five children by then that social services would have split up. On the third day the jury brought in a guilty verdict and the judge ignored their appeal for mercy and sentenced Dorothea to death. An appeal to the Home Secretary was also rejected.

Nottingham Prison no longer had an execution chamber and so Dorothea was transferred to Winson Green Prison in Birmingham to be hanged.

It was executioner Thomas Pierrepoint's last female execution. He was assisted by his nephew Albert, it was his first.

I haven't described the way executions were carried out in this series of books as the procedure was the same each time, so here is the record of Dorothea Waddingham's execution. Be warned, it is not a nice read.

Dorothea was weighed and measured the day before her execution. She was recorded as 4ft 11 inches tall and 123lbs in weight. The executioner then worked out that she would need to drop 8ft 5 inches once the trap door opened to break her neck and bring instant death. On the day of execution she was kept in a cell near or next to the gallows chamber and taken their as quickly as possible at 8am. A white hood was placed over her head and the noose fitted firmly around her neck and the trap door opened, all done in seconds. The prison doctor would then enter the chamber below the gallows and confirm by stethoscope that she was dead. The cell would be cleared of any witnesses and locked for an hour leaving her dangling. Just to be sure. The executioner and his assistant would then enter and pull the body up by using a block and tackle and a rope threaded under her arms. The noose, hood and her clothes would be removed and the body put on a stretcher ready for an autopsy to be carried out. After that Dorothea Waddingham was buried in the prison grounds.

A crowd of 5000 plus anti-capital punishment protesters had gathered outside the prison for Dorothea's execution and sang hymns.

THE END.

Thank you for buying this book. I do hope you enjoyed it as much as I did doing the research. (although perhaps 'enjoy' isn't the right word!) To keep up with my new releases and other information on my talks, what book festivals I am attending and other useless information about me please become a friend on my Barry Faulkner Facebook page. I don't have a website, not enough time, but all my books are on my Barry Faulkner Amazon Books page together with the first pages of each to read. In the UK you can also order them at your local book shop and library if they don't have them already.

DCS Palmer books (crime fiction)

Future Riches
The Felt Tip Murders
Killer is Calling
Poetic Justice
Loot
I'm With The Band
Burning Ambition
Take Away Terror
Ministry of Death
The Bodybuilder
Succession
The Black Rose
Laptops Can Kill
Screen 4
Underneath The Arches

Ben Nevis and the Gold Digger Series (thrillers)

Turkish Delight

National Treasure

Chinese Takeaway

Double Trouble

True Crime Series

London Crime 1930s-2021

UK Serial Killers 1930-2021

UK Killers Vol 1. A to E. 1900-1921

UK Killers Vol 2. F to M. 1900- 2021

UK Killers Vol 3. N to Z 1900-2021

American Killers Vol 1. Alabama

Others

Bidder Beware (Comedy crime)

Fred Karno (biography)

Printed in Dunstable, United Kingdom

81852132R00067